MW00617663

© Avalanche Rescue Fundamentals
Second Edition

© National Ski Patrol System, Inc.
133 South Van Gordon Street, Suite 100
Lakewood, Colorado 80228
303-988-1111
FAX 800-222-4754 or 303-988-3005

Avalanche Rescue Fundamentals
Second Edition

By Dale Atkins and Lin Ballard

The National Ski Patrol (NSP) is a member-driven professional organization of registered ski patrols, patrollers and others, both paid and volunteer. The NSP supports its members through credentialed education and training in leadership, outdoor emergency care, safety, and transportation services, which enables members to serve the community in the safe enjoyment of outdoor recreation.

Project Manager: Mike Laney
Authors: Dale Atkins and Lin Ballard
Editor: Carrie Click
Layout: Alyssa Ohnmacht
Production Coordinator: Denise Cheney
Cover Design: Helen Young, EnZed Design
Cover Photos: Bruce Edgerly, Mike Laney, Steven Reinfurt
Text Illustrations: Dale Atkins, Lin Ballard, Debbie Coleman, Mike Laney

Acknowledgments: We would like to thank the following people for their contributions to this book. Mike Laney provided expertise and guidance throughout the entire process of writing this book. Drew Davis was especially helpful with the Incident Command System chapter. Halsted Morris, Rick Grubin, Henry Ballard and Ed Carlson reviewed the entire text and made many good suggestions, and Patty Burnett contributed her expertise to the rescue dog section.

ISBN 978-0-929752-03-7
Printed in the United States of America
The National Ski Patrol's *Policies and Procedures* manual, as amended, contains the approved national policies of the National Ski Patrol System, Inc. All other publications are educational or informational documents, and may or may not reflect current NSP policies.

TABLE OF CONTENTS

• *Chapter One* •

Overview

Avalanche incidents befall even the most experienced and best-trained sportspeople, and ski patrols and mountain rescue teams have to be ready when trouble strikes. Being ready means having a plan.

Role of organized rescue

At ski areas, avalanche rescue plans must be reevaluated, rewritten and practiced each year as a matter of good management. In the backcountry, mountain rescue teams should also have a written rescue plan that each season is reevaluated, practiced and rewritten as needed. Even backcountry recreationists should have a plan, discussed and practiced amongst friends. Rescues along highways or in towns need additional advance planning with outside agencies, such as the department of transportation and local emergency services.

An important factor that influences plans is attitudes. Today's attitudes about organized avalanche rescue – too late and too slow – are based on circumstances and experiences more than twenty years old. This generational difference creates problems because outdated attitudes guide and affect current avalanche rescue responses. The old attitudes offer no advantages to avalanche victims and rescuers and, in a few cases, have likely harmed avalanche victims.

Opportunities for rescuers to make a difference have changed dramatically, especially in recent years thanks to significant improvements in technologies. In the past decade or so, widespread use of cellular and satellite telephones has significantly changed how quickly rescuers learn of incidents. What used to take hours for someone to report an incident now takes minutes. A generation ago in the United States, rescuers traveled on foot or maybe were aided by a few snowmobiles, and infrequently a helicopter. Today, helicopters are used in nearly half of all avalanche rescues, ferrying in rescuers in minutes. Increasingly, organized rescue teams arrive quickly enough to effectively act as companion rescuers. In a few recent cases, rescue teams have arrived before companions could even start the search for their buried friend.

Search technologies have improved in recent years. Use of transceivers and technology, like the RECCO rescue system, can cut the search time to minutes. Rescue dog teams are increasing in numbers and availability. When considering technologies, rescuers should be less interested in what methods have worked in the past, and more interested in what methods will help them find someone quickly today and tomorrow. Lastly, the quality and availability of medical care both in the field and in the hospital have risen dramatically.

In less than a decade, events and actions that were once barriers to organized rescue teams have now become benefits. It is time for rescuers to embrace a new attitude that organized rescue is effective and can save lives.

Rescue history

The history of avalanche rescue is as old as when people first ventured onto snow-covered mountains. Probably the first organized avalanche rescues took place in late 218 B.C. when Hannibal's army crossed the Alps. According to *The Avalanche Enigma* by Colin Fraser, snow "falling rapidly from the high summits engulfed the living squadrons" and plunged many soldiers into "abysses."

Leaping forward nearly two thousand years to the 1400s, several armies in the Alps were hit by avalanches. And in the late spring of 1800, Napoleon's generals no doubt had to quickly organize rescue efforts when avalanches caught and buried many soldiers as they crossed into Italy. The lessons of avalanche avoidance were not learned, as Napoleon ordered his generals to again take troops over high passes the following November. According to Fraser's *Avalanche Enigma*, avalanches "swallowed whole squadrons."

During World War I, managed and coordinated rescues became a necessity when avalanches killed more than forty thousand soldiers between the Austrian and Italian forces. While natural avalanches killed most, Austrian Army Officer Mathias Zdarsky reported that both sides purposely triggered avalanches as weapons of war.

The roots of organized rescue as performed today can be traced back to Christian Jost, a World War I veteran who, in 1927, founded the Parsenndienst, a Swiss ski patrol above Davos. The Parsenndienst developed a highly trained and professional two-part rescue response – Hasty Party and Main Party – that

became the model for all avalanche rescue in both Europe and North America. By the 1950s, the Parsenndienst had formulated and implemented search techniques, tactics, terminology, and leadership positions that are still used today.

In 1968, based on rescue experiences in the United States and Europe, U.S. Forest Service Snow Ranger Ron Perla introduced a three-stage approach – locate/extricate, administer medical care, and provide operational support – as a logical revision of the classic two-stage rescue response.

In the twenty-first century, another revision has been introduced – coordinating transport, and providing operational support logistics. Today these actions are considered goals that often occur nearly simultaneously rather than as sequential stages. Perhaps the most significant change to rescue management in the U.S. was a Presidential Directive in 2003 that changed the management of all emergency responses – including avalanche – to the Incident Command System (see Chapter 5).

Rescue statistics

The following statistics and summaries are based on information from avalanche incident reports, but a word of caution about these incident statistics is necessary. These data are compiled using avalanche incident reports and news reports. During the past twenty years or so, this data set has become increasingly biased towards avalanche fatalities. This trend has worsened in the past decade, as most reported incidents involve avalanche fatalities with fewer detailed non-fatal incidents being reported. The reader should keep this in mind when interpreting the data. Please spread the word that all incidents should be documented and reported to the Westwide Avalanche Network (avalanche.org), or the Colorado Avalanche Information Center (avalanche.state.co.us). Even small changes in rescue procedures are based on the evaluation of avalanche information gleaned from reports.

Avalanches are insidious killers. Small avalanches can be just as deadly as large avalanches, and both claim lives of the experienced and the novice. The consequences of an avalanche are the same when the danger is low or high. Avalanches are generally a wintertime problem, but avalanches have claimed lives every month of the year. Avalanches are not confined to the high mountains but may lurk on any steep, snow-covered slopes. Close calls and fatal avalanche incidents have occurred in states like Minnesota, Pennsylvania, Missouri and Michigan.

Time

In any avalanche, a buried-avalanche victim's chance of survival diminishes rapidly with increasing burial time, as seen in the Swiss data in Figure 1-1. Time is the enemy of the buried victim.

Though less than one-half of buried victims survive after thirty minutes, some victims do survive for many hours. In favorable circumstances, buried victims can live for hours beneath the snow. The longest burial survivor in the U.S. is about twenty-four hours. This remarkable case occurred in December 2003, when three snowshoers were buried near the Mt. Baker Ski Area in northwestern Washington. Two victims survived burials of nearly twenty-four hours, but sadly, a third companion died.

Burial depth

Many have argued that burial depth is just as important a factor as time because of the crushing weight of the snow; how-

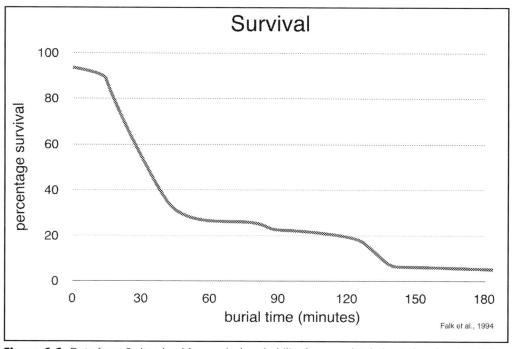

Figure 1-1. Data from Switzerland for survival probability for completely-buried avalanche victims under the snow

ever, there is no statistical evidence of this. The main problem of deep burials appears to be the extra time it takes to reach the buried victim.

In 232 incidents from 1999-2000 to 2008-09, the mean burial depth was 3.8 feet. Interestingly, for survivors, the burial depth was 2.8 feet, but for those killed, the mean burial depth was 4.3 feet. To date, no one in the U.S. has survived a burial deeper than ten feet. However, elsewhere in the world, lucky victims have survived deeper burials. In Switzerland, two mountain guides survived burials of twenty-one and twenty-three feet. Rescuers dug for four hours to uncover the men.

Simple calculations reveal it takes the removal of one to 1.5 tons of snow to excavate a person buried at the average burial depth. Effective and efficient shoveling techniques save time, which may be the difference between life and death. Two such shoveling techniques are described in detail in Chapter 6 and should be used in all digging situations.

Type of rescue

A buried victim's chance for survival relates not only to length of time and burial depth, but also to the type of rescue. Figure 1-2 compiles the statistics on survival as a function of the type of rescue.

Obviously, buried victims rescued by party members or another group nearby the incident site have a much better chance of survival than those found by organized rescue groups – time being the major influencing factor. Of all those found alive, companions rescued 78% while organized rescue parties rescued 12%, which has risen four percentage points in the past several years. This improvement will continue as rescuers are notified sooner, can travel faster, use advanced rescue technologies, and advanced medical care is more available. When Figure 1-2 is read vertically, the statistics are discouraging. Of those "Found by Companions," only 54% (84 of 157) were found alive. To stay alive it's best to not get buried.

Rescue method

Figure 1-3 describes the reported method of rescue for 274 buried avalanche victims during a ten-year period from 1999-2000 to 2008-09. Seventy percent of victims, or thirty-eight of fifty-six people, who were buried with a body part (like a hand or foot) or an attached object (like a ski tip) protruding from the snow were found alive. This statistic shows the advantages of a shallow burial. Of the fatalities in this category, some were skiing alone with no one to spot the hand or ski tip and rescue them. In several other incidents, the search was abandoned prematurely to seek organized rescue. When rescue teams arrived, they found a ski or hand sticking out of the snow.

The avalanche transceiver has been used to find more victims in the past ten years than any other method. The use of transceivers reveals both good news and bad news. Using a transceiver is the best method to find the completely buried victim – if carried and used correctly. The bad news is the mortality rate over the last ten

See Figure 1-2. Type of rescue for buried avalanche victims in direct contact with snow, 1999-2000 to 2008-09 (read left to right)

	Self-rescue	Found by companions	Found by organized rescue team	Total
Alive	11 (10%)	84 (78%)	13 (12%)	108
Dead	—	73 (38%)	119 (62%)	192

Figure 1-3. Method of rescue for buried avalanche victims, 1999-2000 to 2008-09

Method	Found alive	Found dead	Total
Attached object or body part	38	18	56
Spot probe	3	15	18
Coarse or fine probe	1	40	41
Rescue transceiver	39	58	97
Avalanche dog	0	30	30
Voice	7	–	7
Other (digging, RECCO)	2	8	10
Found after a long time span	–	9	9
Not found, not recovered	–	3	3
Inside vehicle	1	0	1
Inside structure	1	1	2
Totals	**92**	**182**	**274**

years is 60%. An avalanche rescue beacon, probe and shovel in trained hands are a buried victim's best hopes for survival, but are still no guarantee of a live recovery.

Not many victims were found by "Voice" (see Figure 1-3) but seven victims shallowly buried were able to yell and be heard by their rescuers. All survived.

The "Other" category includes two victims found alive and four dead by digging, plus three victims found by a RECCO detector. In each of the RECCO cases, the detectors were used long after the incident, or the victim had suffered fatal injuries. Lastly, a magnetometer was used to locate a snowmobile (the rider was next to his machine).

No live "Avalanche dog" rescue was reported in the last ten years despite increasing numbers of trained avalanche-search dogs. In many cases, the dogs arrived at the scene long after the avalanche. Since 1950, there have been six reported live recoveries.

In the category "Not found, not recov-

ered," three victims were never found after being swept into glacial crevasses.

Conclusions

Survival statistics do not favor the buried victim – more will die than will live. A buried victim has only a 34% chance of survival, regardless of all other factors. These statistics are even less optimistic when we consider totally buried victims in direct contact with the snow. By removing from the data samples those victims who were found because of an attached object or body part protruding from the snow, and victims buried within a vehicle or structure, only 24% of totally buried victims survive. Both of these numbers are down about five percentage points during the past five years, which may be due to reporting bias towards mortality or bad luck.

When we consider the large numbers of people exposed to avalanche hazards each winter compared to the annual average number of avalanche fatalities, which stands at twenty-eight in the U.S., there is a low probability that someone will be caught in an avalanche at a given time and location. However, once a person is buried, chances for survival are low – about one in three.

Prevention of incidents is the key to saving lives as no rescue method or device is an adequate substitute for proper route finding and decision making. But when an incident does occur, speed of recovery is still the critical factor in live rescues.

When a buried victim needs more help than his/her companions can provide, organized rescuers must be ready. Time is the enemy of the buried victim, so rescuers must seek opportunities to save time. However, in all incidents, rescuers must weigh their safety with the diminishing probability of finding a live victim. At the same time, no rescue should be abandoned prematurely on the assumption that the victim could not possibly be alive. Worldwide, some victims have been found alive after many hours (even days) and no avalanche victim should ever be denied this small chance at life.

• *Chapter Two* •

Self-Rescue

Although this book is written for the professional rescuer, understanding self-rescue is equally as important as knowing how to rescue others. It is our goal that all those venturing into potential avalanche areas, whether recreationists or professionals, have an understanding of what it takes to survive an avalanche.

Preparation

Preparation includes anticipating potentially dangerous scenarios and responding with appropriate decisions to reduce risks. The best way to reduce risks is by altering plans or routes to avoid periods of increased danger or specific slopes.

However, if these actions are not possible, then special techniques and equipment should be used to mitigate risks:

- Carry and practice using rescue gear.
- Bundle up: zip up your parka, put on hat/helmet and gloves, etc.
- Remove ski leashes and ski pole straps. In addition to an anchoring effect, these items can exert tremendous leverage on extremities and cause severe injury.
- Select an escape route, in case the snow slides.
- Cross as high on the slope as possible and use the same track.
- Cross one at a time, exposing only one person to the danger at a time.
- Cross as quickly and smoothly as possible.

- Stay in visual contact with each person traveling the slope.

Personal rescue equipment

The basics

Every traveler exposed to avalanche danger should be equipped with the core companion rescue equipment: avalanche transceiver, probe and shovel.

Avalanche rescue transceiver

Also called an "avalanche beacon," the transceiver is the most used and most effective rescue tool for locating a buried companion. When used properly, transceivers are fast and effective. All transceivers work on a single world-standard frequency of 457 kHz. When someone is buried, his/her companions switch their devices to "search" and can follow the signal to their buried friend. Newer avalanche transceivers are more user friendly, but they still require regular practice so the user becomes fast enough to save a life. (See Chapter 6, Transceivers.)

Collapsible probe pole

Like a folding tent pole, a collapsible probe is used to pinpoint and confirm a buried victim's precise location. Collapsible probes are effective for companion rescue and for use by an Immediate Search Team in organized rescue. Because

Escape and survival

If you are caught, despite your preparation, there is one basic rule: *Fight for your life!* Depending on the nature of the avalanche and your position in it, you may be able to avoid burial.

Here are a number of actions that may help you fight for your life. And remember, ultimately, fighting for your life means fighting for an air space before the snow stops moving. People who have been buried and lived describe being buried in an avalanche like the feeling of being buried in sand at the beach, and that the only thing moveable is often your toes in your ski boots. The light, fluffy medium sets up quickly. Because you're not able to move, you want your hands in front of your face, creating that essential air pocket.

- Immediately shout to attract the attention of companions.
- Close your mouth to keep from taking in snow.
- Try to stay on your feet as long as possible and follow your escape route.
- Grab onto trees, bushes, rocks, etc. Each second that you hang on lets snow pass by that can't bury you.
- If knocked off your feet, attempt to self-arrest by digging ski poles into the bed surface; if unsuccessful, discard ski poles or other cumbersome gear that might drag you down, hurt you, or make you unable to help yourself. Backpacks should generally be kept securely on your back as they may provide protection and carry items necessary for rescue and survival. Skis with releasable bindings will likely come off, but non-releasable telemark skis, snowboards, and snowshoes may act like anchors.
- Rolling like a log may help you escape to the side.
- To swim or not to swim? Many anecdotal stories tell of victims successfully using swimming motions to escape an avalanche or to reach the surface; however, analysis of avalanche motion and physics suggest that the feasibility and effectiveness of swimming may depend upon where you are in the avalanche and may or may not be helpful. It is most important to fight the avalanche to try to escape. However, as the avalanche begins to slow, the priority shifts to preserving a breathing space instead of continuing a swimming-type motion. Unfortunately, this transition can occur almost instantaneously. Many victims have been trapped with their arms outstretched. That's why there are opposing views on swimming.
- Try facing downhill in a half-sitting position, legs together, in order to minimize injuries resulting from being thrown against rocks and trees.
- If you are under the snow and cannot get to the surface, again, it is critical to position a hand in front of your face before the snow stops. Reaching across to the opposite pack strap or grabbing your parka collar can place your arm in front of your face to make a breathing space.
- If you think you are near the surface, thrust a hand up as the snow stops. This increases the chances of part of your body being above the surface for rescuers to find. It is generally more important, however, to make space to breathe.
- If possible, try to break free as the slide stops and dig yourself out.
- If you are unable to move, do not struggle except to increase the size of the air pocket around your head and face. Conserve your energy. If you hear rescuers directly above you, try shouting. A few victims have been heard and saved. Do not waste too much energy shouting though. Remember, if you are caught in an avalanche, fight for your life! Then, do your best to relax after it stops.

collapsible probes are lightweight and come in different lengths, they are not as well suited for formal probe lines as fixed-length probes.

Shovel

Made from aluminum alloys or Lexan, a high-strength polycarbonate plastic, a small, lightweight and sturdy shovel is essential to uncover a buried person. With the average burial depth of avalanche victims at just over a meter, a rescuer will have to move approximately one ton of hard-packed snow. A shovel is absolutely necessary.

Over the decades, polycarbonate-bladed shovels have been used to dig free many buried avalanche victims; however, there are mounting opinions that these shovels are inferior for use in companion rescue because of the perception that metal-bladed shovels are better. Experience, however, shows that any shovel can be broken if pried upon hard enough to lever out snow – especially those with telescoping handles. Metal-bladed shovels, because they are thinner, work better for chopping into hard snow, which is more likely to be encountered by later-arriving rescuers.

Additional equipment

The following additional devices – listed alphabetically below – can improve rescue and survival. However, none of these items should be used to justify taking additional risks, because surviving any avalanche is uncertain. This equipment should never replace good judgment.

Avalanche airbags

These backpack-carried devices inflate large airbags that tend to keep a person toward the top of a moving avalanche. The airbag works because of the principle of inverse segregation. The process depends on the relative size of particles. A moving avalanche is composed of many different-sized pieces and clumps of snow; gravity causes the smaller particles to fall through the spaces between larger clumps forcing larger clumps upwards. The same process occurs in a bowl of mixed nuts where the big nuts rise to the top, and in a box of cereal where the crumbs settle to the bottom of the box. The airbag makes a person, already a large particle, even larger, making the separation effect even greater. European avalanche researchers Hermann Brugger and Marcus Falk have shown airbags to significantly reduce mortality because airbags help prevent burial.

Avalanche ball

An improved version of the old avalanche cord, the avalanche ball adds a spring-loaded ball tied to the end of a 12-meter cord. Rather than trailed behind, the cord and ball are kept folded up in a small sack that can be attached to a backpack or waist belt. If caught in an avalanche, the user pulls a ripcord deploying the ball, which pops open. The ball tends to stay on the surface and act as a marker allowing companions to quickly follow the cord to the buried victim.

AvaLung™

This simple breathing device is worn either outside clothing like a bandolier or integrated into a backpack. It functions as an artificial air pocket to prolong survival time for a buried person.

If caught in an avalanche, a person can clamp down on the small mouthpiece, ensuring an open airway. If buried, the person draws air through the AvaLung™ from the surrounding snow. The exhaled air, rich in carbon dioxide, is exhausted into another area of the snow reducing the re-inhalation of carbon dioxide. The AvaLung™ has been rigorously tested, and in recent years has been credited with survival in nearly a dozen burials.

Cellular/Mobile and satellite phones

The two-way communication capability of a cellular or satellite phone is critical for alerting rescuers and informing them of the exact nature of the emergency. An avalanche burial or even a suspected burial is a medical emergency, so a call to rescuers should be attempted immediately. Not only can a cellular phone alert rescuers, but the device can also provide location information, helping to pinpoint the caller's location, saving time for responding rescuers.

Many cellular phones can capture and transmit photographs and videos. More and more, 911 call centers are upgrading to handle these files, so rescuers can now also see the problem. While satellite phones may be the most reliable way to communicate from the backcountry, they do not provide location information. In other words, if one calls for rescue, one needs to be able to tell rescuers where to go.

Personal locators

In many backcountry areas, there is no cellular telephone service and satellite telephone service is expensive, so backcountry travelers may want to carry a personal locator beacon (PLB) or a satellite messenger (SPOT) to notify rescuers in the event of an emergency. Both devices have been used successfully, but users must realize that both systems have limitations.

A PLB is a personal radio beacon linked to an array of international search and rescue satellites. When the PLB is activated, the signal is detected by the U.S. Air Force, which notifies state search and rescue officials. Despite being used for decades, there are two principle drawbacks to PLBs: first, the device cannot be tested; second, there is only a distress signal that locates the user. There is no accompanying message about the nature of the emergency.

However, in spring 2010 a new model of PLB has been released that can send a simple "I am OK" message via text message and email.

A popular alternative to PLBs is a satellite messaging system operated by Globalstar Inc. called SPOT. This device and its subscription service uses GPS and satellite communications to alert friends and family that the caller is OK, and to notify friends and family of the caller's location. In the event of a non-life threatening emergency, it also signals that the caller needs some assistance from family or friends (both messages sent by email or by text message), or it transmits a 911 message that one needs the help of a rescue team. The 911 message is monitored by an emergency response center that notifies local search and rescue officials.

Like PLBs, SPOT does not alert rescuers to the nature of the emergency, only that the caller is in need of help. But, unlike older PLBs, SPOT can notify friends and family that the caller is OK, providing peace of mind.

Helmet

Recent North American medical studies reveal a significant number of avalanche victims suffer head injuries. Wearing a helmet may reduce the severity of head injury if caught in an avalanche.

RECCO™ reflectors

While not a tool for self or companion rescue, these small Band-aid-sized passive reflectors integrated into outerwear, boots and helmets allow organized rescue teams to quickly find buried victims. The reflectors are not a substitute for a transceiver, but rather complement transceivers and other technologies. (See Chapter 6, RECCO Avalanche Rescue System.)

• *Chapter Three* •

Companion Rescue

Even though professional rescuers may be better prepared to handle avalanche rescue, many backcountry recreationists face avalanches and other emergencies that occur far out of reach of immediate help. That's why it's important for those venturing into the backcountry to take responsibility for their own safety and for the safety of those in their group, and for professional rescuers to respond as effectively as possible when such an event occurs.

During backcountry trips, it is extremely important to select safe travel routes, use safe travel techniques, and exercise sound judgment at all times. But despite these precautions, backcountry travelers can still encounter serious emergencies.

Some typical emergencies include encountering an avalanche incident, dealing with exhaustion, treating a sick or injured person, having one or more of the party becoming separated from the main group, and equipment failure. If the party is well prepared and equipped to deal with a dangerous situation, it can minimize the potential for an unfortunate outcome.

Preparation

During preparation for a trip, a group should discuss, in depth, a backcountry avalanche rescue plan that identifies the steps to be followed if an emergency occurs. This plan should be a part of the overall trip plan that includes departure and return times, destination, route of travel, alternate routes of travel, overtime allotment (the time after the proposed return before aid should be summoned), etc.

A backcountry plan can be useful. It can be short, but just thinking about a plan can pay off if you ever have to perform a rescue.

Some questions for group members to ask include:

- Who are the people in your party?
- How are they equipped?
- What special skills/capabilities do they possess?
- What are the essential components of an effective rescue and in what order should they be done?

Equipment

At a minimum, everyone in the party should carry an avalanche transceiver, shovel and probe. Avalanche transceivers are the party's best hope of finding a buried person. Everyone in the party should be experienced with transceiver search and strategic shoveling techniques. It is best if the party has practiced as a group.

Probes are needed to confirm the location of a buried person and avoid unnecessary digging. They are also used for spot probing likely burial areas, and in organized probe lines.

Ideally, shovels should be sturdy enough to penetrate compacted snow and large enough to move large volumes of snow speedily. An emergency care kit, survival gear, surveyor tape for marking, and an equipment repair kit are also highly recommended.

Capabilities

Within a backcountry group, members should ask themselves these questions. What are the capabilities of the group? Who has transceiver proficiency, rescue knowledge, first aid and CPR skills, etc.? Who would be the best rescue leader (not necessarily the party leader)? Who's next in line? What equipment is the group bringing on the trip: shovels, probes, transceivers, first aid kit, marking tape? What communications do you have: cell phones, satellite phones, radios? Who knows how to use the phones? Who has avalanche survival equipment (Avalung, airbags, avalanche balls, RECCO reflectors, etc.)? Other information could also prove helpful.

If riding snowmobiles, is there a transportation plan if a driver is incapacitated? Are there spare keys? Is everyone familiar with how to run the snowmobile if one is available?

Organization

Who can take charge when an incident arises? Who knows the critical steps of avalanche rescue? It is vital to have a capable leader who will not panic, can keep the emergency situation in perspective and direct the rescue effort for maximum effectiveness. Every member of a group should be prepared to assume this responsibility if circumstances make it necessary.

Although the *Avalanche Rescue Quick Guide* (an NSP publication) is intended for organized rescue, backcountry users can carry one as an example of rescue planning and as a reminder of search actions. Learning the basics of organized rescue will lead to the most efficient companion rescue.

Avalanche incidents

Minimizing the time of burial is paramount. Remember, recent data analysis suggests that extrication within fifteen minutes may give the buried person about a 90% chance of survival. After that, chances of survival diminish rapidly. Such speed is only possible if the group is prepared and equipped to deal with the emergency. Companions at the site should make every effort to locate the buried person before sending someone away for help.

If the group is equipped with cell phones, radios, etc., try to get outside help as soon as possible, but don't delay initiating the search. However, if dropping below a ridge will mean losing contact, it is better to attempt a 911 call first. The caller should be prepared to give responders a clear description of the incident, the exact location, and the ongoing actions of the survivors. GPS coordinates, if available, are very beneficial, particularly in remote areas. Give all the pertinent information

Figure 3-1. Sample backcountry companion rescue plan

Name	Leader	Specialties	Equipment beyond probe, shovel, beacon	Communication numbers and channels
Name 1	1st	Level 2 Avalanche	Basic first aid kit	Sport radio channel #
Name 2	2nd		AvaLung	Cell #
Name 3		Nurse	Extended first aid kit	Cell #
Name 4		CPR	Repair and survival gear	Sport radio channel #

possible during the initial call as you may lose contact when you move, especially if you drop down into a valley.

The prepared backcountry tour group is already a team. The group is already at the scene and should have been very observant of the incident. Watching carefully when an avalanche occurs and paying attention to where the avalanche is carrying anyone caught, enables companions to concentrate their efforts on the likeliest areas and make the fastest rescue possible. These factors, balanced with good judgment, greatly boost the chances of a live rescue.

Remember that groups traveling in avalanche terrain should stay in visual contact with one another. In one sad incident, a group got separated while traveling to a backcountry hut. The lead person was caught in a small avalanche. When the rest of the group arrived, several minutes later, they very quickly located the person with a transceiver search but were unable to save their companion's life.

Companion rescue actions

If a member of the group is caught in an avalanche, all party members must:

Stop: Focus your attention on the caught companion and the direction and flow of the moving snow.

Look: Watch carefully, noting who is caught, and his/her or her last seen area (LSA). Carefully note landmarks to help you pinpoint the LSA as accurately as possible. Try to spot your companion or other clues like skis, hat, pack, etc.

Listen: Call out and listen for a response. Even if he/she is out of sight, a companion may be only partially buried and able to call out.

Call: Try your cell phone or other communication device to call 911. (But do not waste time – minutes – trying to make the call.)

Organize: Establish a leader to coordinate the rescue.

- Gather survivors for a head count, making sure that everyone is accounted for and there are no overlooked companions who may also have been caught.
- Assess if it's safe to enter the search area; check for hangfire or other potentially hazardous slopes that have the same runout. Determine a safe area for escape and reassembly if another avalanche threatens rescuers.
- Assign specific tasks. Depending on how many companions are available to search, more than one task may be done at the same time, such as transceiver search, surface search and spot probing likely catchments.

Search: Get to work.

- If the party is carrying transceivers, begin a transceiver search from where you enter the debris. Remember to return transceivers back to "transmit" when finished with the transceiver search. (See Chapter 6, Transceiver search.)
- If the party is not carrying transceivers, see Chapter 6 and Chapter 7 for specific techniques and begin the following steps.
- Identify and mark the LSA and direction of the debris flow.
- Continue visual and audible searching. Most people found by these methods survive.
- Make a quick search in line with the LSA along the victim's likely path of travel, based on the debris flow.
- Identify, mark and spot probe all areas around clues.
- Check likely catchment areas (bends, mounds, depressions, rocks and trees) and spot probe these areas.
- Spot probe high-probability deposition areas. If the group is not equipped with commercial avalanche probes, improvise them from anything handy, even tree branches.

- Keep searching. You are the buried person's best hope.
- Establish probe lines only when it is the only option left.

Extricating and providing care
- When a find is made, use as many people as necessary to dig as quickly as possible. (See Chapter 6 for Shoveling techniques, and Triaging multiple burials, below.)
- Use the first part of the victim's body found to estimate the location of his/her head. Go directly to the head and chest, establish an air space and start caring for the person as the rest of the excavation takes place.
- If there are other buried people, resume the search, taking into consideration any new information that comes to light. Finding one person may give a good indication about where to search for others.
- Continue digging to free the victim completely; care for the victim. (See Chapter 9, Extrication and packaging.)

Evacuating

The individual or the group may be able to self-evacuate or may need assistance due to injury or death, missing/broken equipment, darkness or foul weather, or a combination of these factors.

Sometimes, evacuation must wait for help. In that case, make shelter for recovered people. Consider whether you need to stop and make camp for safety if evening is approaching and/or if the weather is deteriorating.

Triaging multiple burials

In organized rescue, there are usually enough personnel and equipment to have one team dig out and care for the first victim located while other teams continue to search for remaining victims. This may not be the case for small groups searching for

missing companions. Having too few rescuers to both uncover a located victim as quickly as possible and continue searching for additional victims at the same time presents a dilemma. Using all available rescuers to dig out the first person found before resuming the search may doom the other buried victim(s). For the lone searcher, the circumstances only magnify the challenge.

Perhaps the most important factor regarding whom to rescue first is the number of rescuers. Certainly, the more rescuers available to search and dig, the easier it will be to make decisions.

There are two situations to consider: multiple rescuers and the solo rescuer.

Multiple rescuers

Several available rescuers allow options. One or more rescuers may stay to dig while others continue the search. Once the victim's head and chest are exposed, one or two rescuers may be released to resume searching for others while one remains behind to finish excavation and render emergency care, if needed. If the victim is unconscious or seriously injured, an additional rescuer, if available, should stay behind to render emergency care. Do not attempt extrication alone.

Solo rescuer

The lone rescuer with several buried victims faces the most difficult of predicaments. Perhaps the worst case is when the first victim located is deeply buried. Should the rescuer mark the spot and move on? Or, does he/she spend the many minutes necessary to uncover the first person but risk taking too long and potentially not saving the other person who may be close by and shallowly buried? Most likely the rescuer will dig the first person out, but in the case of a deep burial, it might be better to mark the spot and move on.

To help make the hard decisions facing

the solo rescuer, consider two factors:
- Proximity of victims
- Burial depths

In reality, the situations and necessary decision making can be far more complex, and there are no easy answers. The rescuer must do the best he/she can, and these simple triage guidelines at least give a starting point.

Consider proximity of victims

Some avalanche transceivers can reveal the number of victims and their approximate distance from the rescuer. If showing only one victim, the logical option is to locate and dig to that person before moving on; however, when victims are close together the solo rescuer may then consider burial depths.

Consider burial depth

If the first victim located is buried deeply, it may be better to mark the spot and move on to the other nearby victim who might be shallowly buried. To dig two meters or more, even to expose the head and chest, takes considerably longer than for someone buried only a meter down.

When you find someone

Be sure to employ a systematic method of digging to minimize shoveling time. (See Chapter 6, Shoveling.) If the victim is conscious and unhurt or suffering minor injuries, he/she may be able to finish digging out while the first rescuer resumes searching. If the victim is breathing but disabled by injury, the rescuer must determine if the injuries are life threatening; if so, care must be rendered before continuing to search for others. If injuries are not life threatening, the rescuer should mark the location and may temporarily leave the victim to search for others. If the victim is not breathing, the rescuer should clear the victim's airway, head and chest, then

attempt rescue breathing twice; if the victim does not start breathing on his/her own, position the victim with an open airway, mark the location, and continue the search for the remaining victim(s).

The victim's beacon: Turn off or leave on?

When multiple victims are known, conventional wisdom indicates it is best to turn off each found-victim's transceiver so not to interfere in the search of others. However, reviews from rescues suggest that many additional minutes are spent clearing snow just to reach the transceiver. In a series of trials conducted by Manuel Genswein of Switzerland and Ragnihild Eide of Norway, the delays were confirmed, sometimes averaging more than ten additional minutes: time that could have been used to search for and maybe uncover another victim. Their work demonstrates the importance of being able to keep searching without turning off the beacon of previously located victims.

> **TIP:** Any time an injured or incapacitated victim is left alone, use a ski, ski poles, the victim's pack, etc. to mark the location so that it can be seen at a distance, even when the victim's transceiver is left on transmit.

Going for help

The above should emphasize the need for companions to remain at the scene to help with search and rescue. If 911 calls do not go through, and search results indicate that additional help is needed, you must determine when to go for help. There is no clear answer. Consider going for help when you have done everything possible, then send two people together while the rest keep searching or caring for injured people. Go only as far as needed to establish communications. Be sure that those going for help know how to give the exact location and pertinent details of the incident. Marking the egress route will make it easier to find the way back.

A more in-depth discussion of Immediate Search procedures can be found in Chapter 7. See Chapter 6 for a detailed explanation of Rescue Techniques and Technologies.

Spontaneous arrival of others

In some instances, individuals or members of other groups happen upon the scene of a companion rescue. It is vital the groups merge and coordinate their efforts as quickly as possible. A main stumbling block often deals with leadership, and more often than not the issue is not one of too many leaders but one of no leader.

Most groups are eager to help. The only rule is to approach the accident safely so as not to trigger a second avalanche. Beyond this basic rule, here are some suggestions.

Arriving group

If the arriving group observes a fairly well-organized companion search underway, they should immediately offer help. The companions already on scene know more about the circumstances of the incident. Incoming rescuers need to find out what has been done, what needs to be done and what might need to be redone, and offer suggestions.

If the arriving group observes a disorganized effort, the arriving group needs to take charge, even if it is only amongst the incoming rescuers. Try to work with or around the original group as best as you can, given the circumstances.

Companion search group

If the companion search leader observes an approaching group, he or she should quickly ask about any special skills or equipment the group might have. Quickly inform the new group about the state of the rescue, ask if they are willing to help, and give them assignments.

• *Chapter Four* •

Organized Rescue Planning

Whether in (or near) a ski resort or in the backcountry, a rescue plan is needed to steer the rescue operation. This is sometimes referred to as a pre-plan, which is a general plan that guides the rescue, as compared to the tactical plan that is created for a specific rescue operation.

In order for ski patrols and mountain rescue teams to conduct an effective organized rescue, it is important to fully understand all the components of avalanche rescue that are typically carried out with abundant personnel and well-placed equipment.

An organized on-area (or near-area) rescue depends on developing and practicing a rescue plan before the incident occurs. The rescue plan is a written plan of action that will be used in any avalanche incident at or near the area. It is updated as needed; however, it should be reviewed annually before the season begins. Regular testing by practicing the procedures via simulated rescues will increase the plan's effectiveness and efficiency. Rescue plans should be reevaluated on the basis of recent experience, new lifts, new personnel, new areas, and additional equipment.

The plan is precise about:
• how rescuers are notified
• how rescuers should respond
• who fulfills key leadership positions, how to contact them, and their responsibilities
• where equipment is cached and how it will be managed

• how to contact supporting agencies and other resources

Rescue plan goals

Formerly, we referred to rescue "stages," a term that was often misinterpreted as a serial approach to rescue. These are now considered rescue "goals" as they can be initiated simultaneously.

They include:
• **Immediate Search** – Get rescuers to the site; find and uncover the victims
• **Medical** – Provide care for the victims
• **Transport/Evacuation** – Get the victims out of the field and to advanced care if needed
• **Support/Logistics** – Care for the rescuers in the field (food, shelter, rest and replacements)

Immediate Search

Immediate Search involves the speedy dispatch of teams equipped with rescue transceivers, probes, shovels, light equipment for emergency care, and personal emergency gear. If possible, a dog team, RECCO detectors, and a witness should accompany one of the Immediate Search teams. The objective of the Immediate Search Teams is to locate and uncover the victim(s). These rescuers are not equipped for a prolonged operation; they travel fast and light to the incident site and leave as soon as possible.

Medical

Avalanche incidents almost always include medical emergencies, so Medical Team(s) must be assembled and dispatched as soon as possible. Although rescuers in Immediate Search Teams carry standard emergency care kits (often containing oxygen) to deal with initial problems, they cannot be slowed down in order to transport bulkier equipment needed for continued resuscitation and other medical care.

Special teams of three to seven rescuers (including a physician or paramedic, if possible) are organized to transport toboggans, blankets, sleeping bags, resuscitation and trauma equipment needed to revive and stabilize victim(s). For out-of area rescues additional gear such as a tent, stove and other equipment may be needed.

As soon as the alarm is received, the Incident Commander (see description, page 19) should appoint a person to organize the Medical Team(s) and collect the necessary equipment. Ideally, the Medical Team(s) leave just behind the Immediate Search Teams.

Transport/Evacuation

Rapid transport to advanced medical care is usually critical for an avalanche victim. The Incident Commander (IC) may put a helicopter or ambulance on standby as soon as the incident is reported. A toboggan is usually sent to the Incident Site to transport medical equipment in and victims out. Arrangements for transport depend on the condition of the victims and the transport options available. Options to consider include snowmobiles, snowcats, helicopters, etc. In some instances, special evacuation/extrication equipment and expertise may be required.

Support

The extent to which support is needed will vary widely according to the size of the incident, weather conditions, terrain problems, and the progress of the rescue. In some cases, it may not be necessary. In other cases, this may be the largest time and manpower component of the operation. Support includes contacting additional personnel and transporting them into the field, and providing food, shelter, rest and replacement for rescuers. Appendix A contains a list of suggested support equipment.

Communications

Because avalanche search and rescue requires quick action by many rescuers and different agencies, a well thought-out communications plan is essential. Early season planning sessions with leaders of nearby ski patrols, rescue teams, law enforcement, and emergency service programs allows for review of the rescue plan and provides the opportunity to discuss how best to communicate. These meetings also give rescuers from different organizations the opportunity to meet one another face-to-face, which proves invaluable when meeting again during a rescue.

During any search and rescue effort, effective communications are critical to the success of the operation. Many minds need to act as one – focused on the rescue's objectives and the safety of personnel working in the field. Common terminology, common communication, and the willingness of all parties to provide specific, targeted information are vital.

Communications, especially telecommunications, need to convey only essential information, at the right time and to the right people. To reduce misunderstandings, it is important that communication is collaborative: two-way with some feedback or response given. Taking time to establish reliable communications at the beginning of an operation saves time in terms of overall efficiency and effectiveness. Generally, a search and rescue operation that starts well ends well; one that starts poorly organized and coordinated tends to be very difficult to get back in control. The quality and extent of communication between rescue leaders and rescue workers makes the difference.

Leadership positions

Incident Commander

The Incident Commander (IC) is the overall coordinator of the rescue operation. This person should have strong management skills, avalanche rescue knowledge, and be thoroughly familiar with the rescue plan and the area. In some instances, typically in the backcountry, the agency having jurisdiction (e.g. sheriff's office, state police, or Park Service) will designate the IC. If there is a transition of command to a new IC, it is recommended that the previous IC be assigned some role on the incident. In many cases, the previous IC becomes the Operations Section Chief or assumes some other tactical leadership role.

There should always be one person on duty qualified to perform this role. The rescue plan should contain a resource list identifying qualified Incident Commanders and their contact information. An important portion of the rescue plan is a listing of the steps necessary to initiate an initial avalanche incident response.

Immediate Search Team Leader

The Immediate Search Leader is often in charge of determining a safe route into the Incident Site and marking the route for follow-up teams. The Immediate Search Team Leader is temporarily in charge at the Incident Site until a Site Leader takes over. This individual must be trained and experienced in avalanche hazard assessment and safe travel in avalanche terrain.

Site Leader

In this book, we use the term Site Leader to clarify that this is the leader in charge at the avalanche. In the Incident Command System, (see Chapter 5), this person could have the title of IC, Operations Chief, Rescue Group Leader, etc., depending upon the size and complexity of the operation. We attach the word "site" to the Incident Command System titles.

The Site Leader is a qualified, designated person who takes over management of the rescue effort at the site. Often not available immediately, the Site Leader is sent to the Incident Site as quickly as possible and relieves the person in charge (possibly the Immediate Search Team Leader). The Site Leader evaluates the actions of those already on the scene and decides where and how to search and what other resources are needed.

Team Leaders

Team leaders are experienced rescuers who can lead groups of three to seven rescuers to the Incident Site quickly and safely. Depending on the number of resources they are assigned, they may have ICS titles of Crew Supervisors, Strike Team or Task Force Leaders. They are responsible for screening personnel, equipping the team, and letting the Incident Dispatcher know that the team is ready to head out. For speed, safety and accountability purposes, the Team Leader provides the Staging Manager or Incident Dispatcher with a roster of personnel and equipment taken before departing. (See Appendix, Sample Team Roster.) They report to the Site Leader.

Special Roles
Incident Dispatcher

Even though there may be a ski area or agency dispatcher, consider appointing a separate Incident Dispatcher dedicated to the rescue effort. This person works closely with the IC to manage and track communications. A voice recorder can be beneficial if available. The IC may direct the Incident Dispatcher to make necessary calls and contacts. A Dispatch Log should be kept of all communications. This person may also take over some or all of the responsibilities of the Scribe as directed by the IC. (See Appendix, Sample Dispatch Log.)

Scribe

A Scribe is almost always assigned to the IC and often to Section Chiefs or the Site Leader to document the activities of that position. This documentation is essential for tracking, controlling and accounting for the planning, decision-making, and execution of the operation. (See Appendix, Sample Scribe Notes.)

Other ICS positions fill out the Command and General Staff depending on the size and complexity of the incident as described in Chapter 5, Introduction to ICS:
- Safety Officer
- Public Information Officer
- Liaison Officer
- Logistics Chief
- Planning Chief
- Operations Chief

Generalized rescue plan

This is not a sequential list of actions; some may be organized and performed simultaneously. The plan should describe flexible processes and protocols that allow for modification to fit the conditions of each incident.

Report incident
- Interview witness (see Appendix, Sample Witness Interview Sheet)
- If witness(es) physically present, appoint a person to hold and continue interviewing witness(es)

Alert and respond
- Notify Rescue Headquarters

- Agency dispatcher notifies rescuers
- Rescuers respond per avalanche rescue pre-plan
- IC is designated; he/she assumes command and implements ICS as needed (see Appendix, Sample IC Checklist/Data Form)
- Appoint Incident Dispatcher and Scribe as needed
- Dispatch initial Immediate Search Team (including witness, dog team, and RECCO detector if available)
- Coordinate initial travel logistics as needed (initial assessment of safe route, route marking, etc.)
- Dispatch a Site Leader
- Dispatch the Medical Team
- Dispatch additional teams

Locate/Extricate
- Immediate Search Team assesses scene safety and initiates search
- Incorporate additional resources (teams and technology) into search effort as they arrive
- As soon as located, dig out victim(s) as expeditiously as possible
- When extricating, assume possible spine injuries unless they can be specifically ruled out

Provide medical care
- Provide Basic Life Support (and Advanced Life Support if available)
- Protect victim(s) from further injury or cooling

Treat victim(s)
- Prepare victim(s) for transport
- Continually monitor victim(s)

Evacuate victim(s)
- Move victim(s) to a safer area if necessary
- Move victim(s) to a helicopter landing spot, or other place for additional care

Support

- Prepare for a longer running operation
- Arrange for additional searchers
- Arrange for additional equipment
- Arrange to care for rescuers

Documentation

The need to start an early and thorough documentation of the rescue process cannot be overstated. Effective plans will have forms and checklists to guide and document every component of the rescue operation. They help ensure that important details are not overlooked, that vital functions are properly managed, and that simultaneous actions are coordinated. They are necessary for the legal and fiscal accountability that will follow the rescue, regardless of operational outcome.

Each agency having jurisdiction will have procedures for documenting and reporting an avalanche incident. A model incident reporting form can be found in *Snow, Weather, and Avalanches: Observational Guidelines for Avalanche Programs in the United States,* produced by the American Avalanche Association and the USDA Forest Service National Avalanche Center. Reporting incidents is important for gathering statistics and for learning that will enhance future rescue operations. Other sample forms and checklists may be found in the Appendices of this book.

Equipment

One of the essentials for a speedy rescue is to have equipment fully organized and ready for distribution before any alarm is sounded. There are many different ways to organize equipment caches, depending on the layout of the ski area. Exact details should be specified in the rescue plan. The plan also specifies a way to track equipment, check it in and out, and put it back in service.

In general, a major cache containing equipment for all rescue needs should be maintained at a strategic location. Small caches containing equipment for Immediate Search Teams should be set up at lift terminals or in the vicinity of potential slide paths. (See Appendix, Sample Equipment List.)

Customizing a rescue plan

The most important step in preparing a rescue plan is taking the generic rescue plan and incorporating specific area procedures, personnel, and equipment. Various alterations to the generic plan may become evident through the application of local logic. For example, some areas have designated Staging Areas for rescuers to report to when an alarm is sounded. Incorporating non-rescue personnel at the area into the plan can greatly aid in the rescue. Lift operators may get the first report. Ski instructors and other area personnel can be used in rescue and non-rescue roles.

Other features of a plan might include safe travel procedures related to local terrain, the availability of snowmobiles, snowcats, helicopters, or the presence/absence of avalanche control capabilities. Pre-marked maps showing known slide paths, routes into areas, prevailing winds, location of equipment caches, etc. are a good addition to the plan and can be placed in duty stations.

Clearly, annual or more frequent evaluation of plans is critical. Changes continually occur in the many variables (procedures, personnel, equipment, trail layout, food services, etc.) that affect the protocols developed for handling emergency operations. All area personnel who may be involved in a rescue operation should know the plan. If possible, try to arrange some practices that include outside agencies that are likely to respond to an incident at or near your area. Brainstorming, simulation, and practice all contribute in creating the most effective rescue plan.

• *Chapter Five* •

Incident Command System

In 2003, the Department of Homeland Security implemented the Presidential Directive 5, a national management system that uses the same terminology and incident command procedures in dealing with natural and manmade disasters and emergencies.

Called the National Incident Management System (NIMS), all domestic incidents managed by federal, state, local and private and nongovernmental sectors are mandated to use what is called the Incident Command System (ICS). To enforce the use of ICS, NIMS requires that all agencies at all levels adopt ICS as a condition to receive federal preparedness Homeland Security funding.

Most public safety agencies can arrange basic ICS trainings for local rescue teams and ski patrols. More information can be found at the end of this chapter. Additionally, the *ICS Field Operations Guide* is an essential tool for each person filling a leadership role in an ICS organization.

Developed by the Fire Scope Project, a cooperative effort of federal, state and local agencies in Southern California in the early 1970s for fighting fires, ICS has been adapted widely by many agencies and organizations that routinely confront rapidly developing emergencies: fire, hazardous materials spills, search and rescue, etc. These are emergencies that require resources from many organizations that may be unfamiliar with each other, but must work together.

ICS benefits avalanche search and rescue because the system:
- provides objectives that determine how the rescue will be managed
- can be initiated at any time in the operation
- is capable of growing and contracting with the size of the operation (incident)
- encourages the leaders to delegate responsibility, enabling them to maintain an overall perspective of the operation
- limits the "span of control" of any one individual from three to seven subordinates total, therefore reducing the potential for miscommunication
- permits modular organization (one person or group each handles operations, planning, logistics, finances, etc.), to avoid overloading anyone with too many areas of responsibility
- tracks costs incurred during the operation (an important concern for ski areas and law enforcement personnel)
- allows for a unified command (permitting more than one agency to provide input into the management of the operation)
- provides documentation of activities with a series of forms that already have been modified for search and rescue activities
- uses common terminology (a benefit when working with agencies that have little or no avalanche rescue experience)

Avalanche rescuers must organize their operations according to the principles and practices of ICS. This facilitates the integration of rescue efforts with other agencies. ICS provides an umbrella management system that is discipline neutral. ICS qualifications and titles do not correlate with local management titles. For example, someone who holds the title of "chief" in everyday work may not hold that title in ICS. The reason is to avoid any potential confusion with other position titles, management styles, and organizational structures.

Management functions

The foundation of ICS is based on five major management functions or responsibilities. These five functions apply to all incidents from routine rescues to mass disasters.

Incident Command/Incident Commander (IC) has the overall authority and responsibility for the incident, and sets the incident objectives, strategies, and priorities.

Operations conducts activities to reach the incident objectives. Operations establishes the tactics and directs all operational resources.

Planning supports the incident-action planning process by tracking resources, collecting and analyzing information, demobilizing resources and managing the incident's documentation.

Logistics provides resources and services to support the achievement of the incident objectives.

Administration/Finance provides accounting and monitors costs related to the incident.

Position titles

Supervisory titles in ICS are shown below. They are standardized to help avoid confusion when different agencies are involved. More detailed descriptions of their specific avalanche rescue duties and responsibilities can found in Chapter 4.

ICS organizational components

Awareness of the following components is vital for implementing ICS in avalanche rescue.

Incident Commander (IC)

This is the only position always staffed in ICS responses. On small incidents, the IC may be responsible for the following management functions until he/she delegates the function to others.

Command staff

This staff consists of the Public Information Officer, Safety Officer, and Liaison Officer. Each is designated as an Officer and may have Assistants as needed.

Figure 5-1. Major management functions of ICS

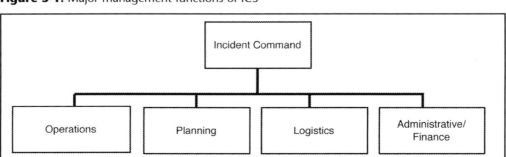

Public Information Officer

This person may:

- meet with the media
- establish place(s) and time(s) for press briefings
- prepare information for release, after approval by the IC
- coordinate information releases with other agencies or organizations

Ski resorts and law enforcement agencies usually have individuals trained for this function.

Safety Officer

This officer identifies hazardous situations associated with the incident and mitigates unsafe conditions, operations, or hazards. The Safety Officer can alter, suspend, or terminate activities that pose a danger to rescuers. In avalanche incidents this person may:

- track weather conditions
- consult with the local avalanche center
- coordinate with Safety Assistant(s) at the site

Liaison Officer

In a large avalanche incident with many rescue teams, this person is the point of contact for coordinating with other agencies and rescue organizations.

General Staff (Sections)

These organizational levels have responsibility for a major functional area of the incident response (e.g., Operations, Planning, Logistics, Finance/Administration). The person in charge of each Section is designated as a Section Chief. Early in the response or during small incidents, the IC may be responsible for section functions until those functions are delegated to others.

Operations Chief

He/She directs the field search and rescue activities.

Planning Chief

He/She tracks personnel and equipment and maintains documentation.

Logistics Chief

He/She provides resources and needed services – rescuers, equipment, food, shelter, etc.

Administrative/Finance Chief

He/She provides accounting related to the incident.

The members of the Command and General Staffs typically perform their duties at the Incident Command Post with the possible exceptions of the Incident Commander and Operations Chief who both may work at the Incident Site, either early on or in the case of small incidents.

Branch

This term is used when the number of Divisions or Groups exceeds the span of control. It is either geographical or functional. The person in charge of each Branch is designated as a Director.

Division

In avalanche response, Divisions are used to divide the site geographically, e.g., a very large or a long debris area, or an avalanche with multiple runout zones. The person in charge of each Division is designated as a Division Supervisor.

Group

Groups describe functional areas of responsibilities. An example of a Group in avalanche rescue might be the Medical Group. The person in charge of each Group is designated as a Group Supervisor.

Task Force

A Task Force is a combination of resources with different capabilities and with common communications operating under the direct supervision of a Task Force Leader.

Strike Team

A strike team consists of a set number of resources with the same capabilities and with common communications operating under the direct supervision of a Strike Team Leader. Avalanche rescuers typically have multiple capabilities and equipment, so they are not defined as having one function. However, in a large avalanche incident, resources, such as probe lines, may be designated as Strike Teams to assist with managing large numbers of people.

Unit

This term is used for a specific incident planning, logistics, or finance/administration organizational entity but not for an operation. For example: Food Unit, Communications Unit, Documentation Unit, etc.

Single Resource

A Single Resource describes an individual piece of equipment and the personnel required to operate it, or an established crew or team of individuals with an identified work supervisor that can be used on an incident.

Crew

A grouping of Single Resources.

Resources

These are available or potentially available personnel and equipment.

Technical Specialist

An individual with specialized skills or knowledge assigned wherever their skills are required.

Incident Action Plan

The Incident Action Plan (IAP) includes the objectives reflecting the strategy, tactics, and supporting information. The plan may be oral – typical in the initial response phase of incidents – or written, in larger, complex incidents.

Jurisdiction

Most avalanche incidents occur within a single jurisdiction. The agency having jurisdiction (AHJ) is a county sheriff, or in some states, the state police, and in some national parks, the park service. For avalanche rescues outside of ski resorts and in the backcountry the AHJ will designate a single Incident Commander.

Some avalanche incidents are "multi-jurisdictional." Examples include a county and a national park or two adjoining coun-

Figure 5-2. ICS supervisory titles

Organizational level	Title	Subordinate's title
Incident Command	Incident Commander (IC)	Deputy
Command Staff	Officer	Assistant
General Staff (Section)	Chief	Deputy
Branch	Director	Deputy
Division/Group	Supervisor	N/A
Unit	Leader	Manager
Strike Team/Task Force	Leader	Single Resource Supervisor

ties. These situations may be managed using a Unified Command structure. Unified Command provides for an Incident Commander from each jurisdiction and for the development of a single Incident Action Plan. When multi-jurisdictional incidents are possible, pre-planning meetings and joint training with requisite jurisdictions and rescue teams will ensure smoother performance during rescues.

Implementing ICS

In ICS and in avalanche rescue, the first person receiving the report of an avalanche incident becomes the Incident Commander (IC) until the IC responsibility is transferred to another individual(s). In an incident reported within a ski area, the emergency call is often transferred to a ski patrol dispatcher who alerts the designated IC according to the area's avalanche rescue pre-plan.

ICS does not affect the tactical approach of how an avalanche rescue is performed; ICS only guides how the incident is organized and managed. The functional activities of avalanche rescue remain the same.

Always remember that small and simple incidents should be managed with a small and simple command structure. The Incident Commander should only delegate responsibility when needed as the incident's complexity increases. See Figure 5-3.

Figure 5-3. Simple response involving two to seven rescuers

Incident types

Incidents are "typed" as to their complexity and the capabilities of the leaders to manage the incident. A local ski patrol or mountain rescue team typically initiates an avalanche rescue. As the complexity in the response increases due to increasing resources or the magnitude of the incident, higher trained management with more capabilities are needed. Management teams and incidents are "typed" in five levels from Type 5 (least complex) to Type 1 (most complex).

Type 5

Type 5 incidents are managed with a minimum number of resources from a single ski patrol or mountain rescue team following their avalanche rescue plan. No written ICS Incident Action Plan is needed and the duration is a few hours (a Single Operational Period). There are a limited number of Single Resources composed of single individuals or Crews with a leader. The Incident Commander is typically located on the Incident Site and provides all tactical direction and incident management.

A simple and idealized ICS response, using Groups to manage span of control within the Operations Section, is presented in Figure 5-4. In this example, the IC is performing the Operations function as well as the Planning, Logistics, and Finance/Administrative functions, which are minimal.

The IC has organized the Operations functions into Groups and assigned Group Supervisors who will manage other rescuers. Though not shown in Figure 5-4, the IC may also appoint a Safety Officer, particularly when snow or weather conditions are hazardous or changing rapidly. Other organizational schemes for this type of incident are possible using ICS. The result of reaching the span of control limits means the IC may need to delegate the Operations Functions. When this occurs,

Figure 5-4. An example of a Type 5 incident response

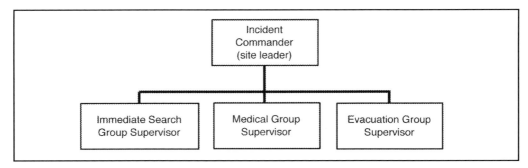

the IC delegates the operations responsibilities to an Operations Section Chief.

Type 4

More complex than the Type 5 incident, a Type 4 incident (Figure 5-5) typically requires additional resources and management personnel. Additional resources may come from neighboring ski resorts and nearby rescue teams. The IC may or may not be located at the Incident Site. A dedicated manager – site leader – will be assigned to manage the operations at the Incident Site. Some Command or General Staff positions may be filled to manage safety issues, media demands, and incoming rescue teams.

No written ICS Incident Action Plan is needed, though the operation briefing may be documented to aid in briefing incoming resources. Additional management positions are filled to maintain span of control limits or assist the IC with managing workload demands. This management configuration may be implemented for a single operational period (typically twelve

Figure 5-5. An example of a Type 4 incident response

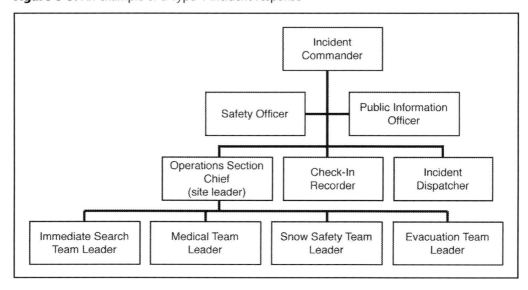

Figure 5-6. An example of a Type 3 incident response

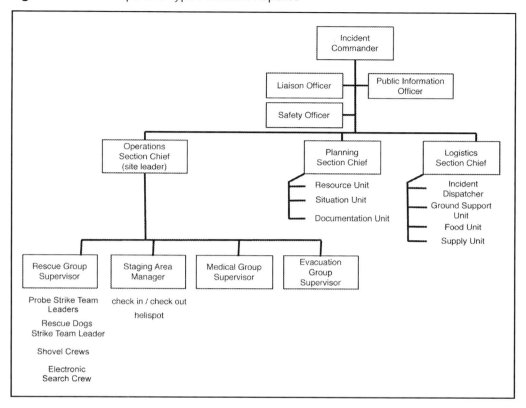

hours) or during multiple operational periods with a limited number of resources assigned.

Type 3

At the Type 3 level of complexity (Figures 5-6 and 5-7), the incident has not been resolved during the first operational period. The complexity increases with increasing numbers of Resources, which requires additional tactical management and supporting personnel. Tactical Resources may be organized as Single Resources, Strike Teams, or Task Forces. Multiple Command and General Staff positions are filled as needed to manage span of control and workload. At this level of complexity a formal incident planning

process is implemented resulting in the production of a written Incident Action Plan.

Type 2 and 1

These are very large and complex incidents involving resources from across the United States. An avalanche incident requiring this sort of response is unlikely, but a Type 2 incident may be possible if, for example, a large mass-casualty incident occurred, such as a large avalanche or several avalanches hitting a town. Type 1 responses are often designated for incidents affecting several states like floods, tornadoes and hurricanes.

Figure 5-7. An example of a Type 3 incident response with avalanche debris divided into two Divisions

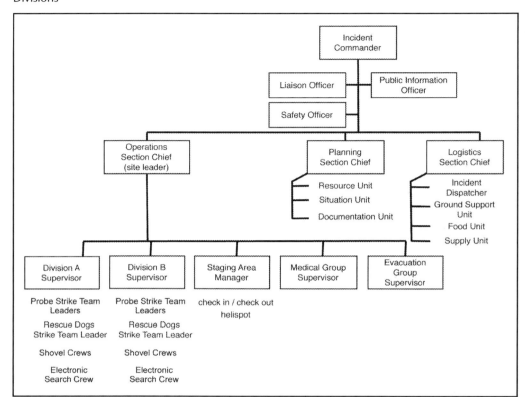

ICS training

The Department of Homeland Security mandates that emergency responders successfully complete basic ICS and National Incident Management System (NIMS) trainings.

Fortunately, the Federal Emergency Management Agency (FEMA) makes much of the training and certification available online through the national Emergency Management Institute (EMI). For most rescuers – ski patrollers and mountain rescuers – the following courses should be taken:

- ICS-100, Introduction to Incident Command System
- ICS-200, ICS for Single Resources and Initial Action Incidents

- IS-700.a, NIMS An Introduction
- IS-800.b, National Response Framework, an Introduction

Each course can be taken in the classroom or by online independent study, in several hours, at training.fema.gov.

In addition to the above courses, for middle management positions, rescuers should also take ICS-300; and for top management positions (Command and General Staff), rescuers should take ICS-400. These two courses are state administered classroom programs. For additional information on these courses, rescuers should contact their state emergency management agency.

• *Chapter Six* •

Rescue Techniques and Technologies

To maximize the chances of finding a victim in time to save his/her life, rescuers must identify and evaluate the areas in which the victim is most likely buried, and then prioritize those areas for searching.

Where to search

In most cases, the moving avalanche carries the victim(s) down the flow line from the last seen area (LSA) to the places of greatest

Figure 6 2. Catchments

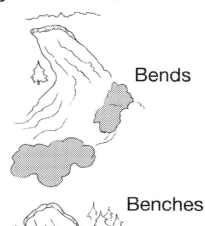

Bends

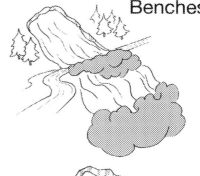

Benches

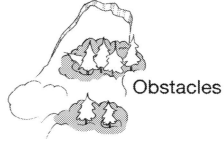

Obstacles

Figure 6-1. Estimate of likely burial based on entry, LSA and debris flow

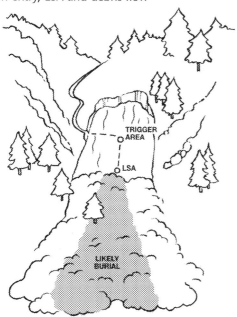

snow deposition, perhaps near the down-slope end, or toe, of the debris. If possible, view the avalanche debris from the top. This perspective gives one a good idea of the flow of the avalanche. If this is not possible, determine flow from whatever vantage point may be available. Figure 6-1 indicates a likely burial area based on visual sighting and flow.

Be alert to terrain traps where victims are often snared by rocks, trees, benches and depressions in the terrain (catchments). Remember too that victims can end up in creek bottoms and lakes. If an avalanche follows a wandering gully, all areas of deposition are likely burial places, particularly the outside corners of bends. Again, the victim is likely to be where the greatest amount of snow is deposited, unless clues indicate otherwise.

Figure 6-3. Likely burial area based on trajectory and catchments

Expect the unexpected

The victim may be thrown out of a slide, moved out of the debris, or get tossed into a tree. Keep this in mind while searching the avalanche. In one instance, a young boy escaped burial in the avalanche but died from hypothermia in the woods while rescuers carefully probed the avalanche debris. There are unusual cases where victims have been pushed under the seemingly undisturbed snow just beyond the perimeter of avalanche debris.

Modern snowmobiles with their high-performance engines and paddle-like tracks sometimes allow riders to escape as their machines churn across the avalanche. Unlucky riders hidden by moving snow or powder clouds may end up some distance away from where they were last seen, misleading rescuers who search directly downslope of the LSA.

How to search

There are many techniques and technologies that are useful for rescue. They can be employed simultaneously during the search, depending on the area of the incident, and the equipment and number of victims and searchers.

Some common techniques and technologies are:
- visual and audible search
- clue handling and marking
- transceivers
- spot probing
- perimeter search
- dogs
- RECCO
- probe lines
- strategic shoveling
- helicopters
- GPS

Visual and audible search

A visual search begins during the approach, even before entering onto the debris. It yields important first impressions of the nature of the incident and indicates how to start the search. The entire debris area should be searched visually and audibly for the victim. The visual search should include looking for tracks in and out of the area, identifying LSA(s) looking for clues, and noting the flow of the avalanche.

Rescuers should call out the victims' names and listen for responses or cries for help. Not many victims have been found by voice but those who have been found by this method have a high survival rate.

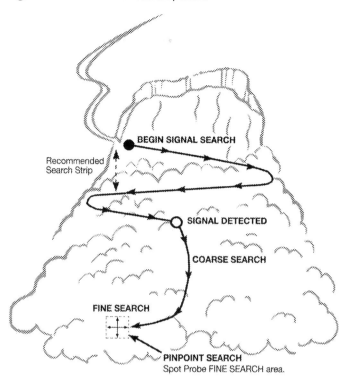

Figure 6-4. Transceiver search phases

BEGIN SIGNAL SEARCH

Recommended Search Strip

SIGNAL DETECTED

COARSE SEARCH

FINE SEARCH

PINPOINT SEARCH
Spot Probe FINE SEARCH area.

TIP: There have been recent incidents when survivors, feeling helpless and in a panic, hurried off to get help. When the rescue team arrived, a visual search quickly located the victim. Sadly, it was too late to recover the person alive. If the survivors had done a visual search, their companions might have been uncovered immediately.

It is important for rescuers to continue visual and audible searching throughout the operation no matter what other methods they may be using. Remember that from different parts of the debris, the view and perspective changes. Searchers doing other jobs like spot probing or transceiver searching can get distracted, overlook clues, and forget to be quiet and listen.

Clue handling

Any object or hint of where a victim may be buried should be checked, marked, reported to your leader, and if appropriate, the area should be spot probed. Clues can be tracks into the avalanche or out of the debris, items of clothing, or equipment. Items like gloves, skis and ski poles may still be attached to the person so check before moving the clue. Clues should be marked and left securely in place. The international marking system has designated the color blue for clues. Try to identify to whom each clue belongs. It is helpful to

Figure 6-5. Signal search pattern for a wide path with few searchers available

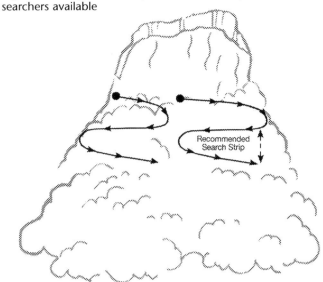

Recommended
Search Strip

dure for using their transceivers and practice on a regular basis.

The goal of the transceiver search in organized rescue is to quickly and thoroughly search the debris to either find the buried victim or to rule out that the victim had a transceiver.

Four phases of a search: (See Figure 6-4)

Signal search – (find the signal)

Coarse – (get close)

Fine – (narrow the final location)

Pinpoint – (locate with a probe)

mark clues belonging to the same victim in a way that can be distinguished from other victims. This may be accomplished by a second flag of another color or adding surveyor tape to the flag, etc.

> **TIP:** Make sure that all clues are reported. Remember that there are many demands on leaders so do not give up. Get all pertinent information passed along and get acknowledgement.

Transceivers

A transceiver is the most effective avalanche rescue device currently available. Every avalanche rescue worker and all members of groups who travel in avalanche country should carry one. Some ski areas require guests to wear a transceiver before skiing certain parts of the terrain.

Transceivers offer speedy detection. In most cases, the victim can be found within minutes after the signal is first picked up, providing rescuers know the correct proce-

Preparation

When rescuers are safely on the debris and ready to search, determine how many rescuers are needed to cover the area. Appoint rescuers to do the transceiver search and have them switch to "receive." All others switch to "off." When many searchers are present and the search area is small, limit the number of searchers doing the transceiver search. Too many searchers with audible transceivers can increase the noise level and cause interference with other searchers.

Signal search

Arrange spacing according to manufacturer's specifications for optimum search strip widths. When there are few rescuers, use a zigzag pattern. There are a number of patterns that can be used to accomplish the signal search. When many rescuers are available, use lines or a mix of patterns to cover the area. With a large number of rescuers, available rescuers can search in parallel aligned closer than the recommended search strip widths.

Organizing a larger group takes time, so send a single rescuer (or several) ahead to quickly initiate the immediate search for a beacon signal or other clues.

Begin the search where you enter the debris, i.e., if the approach is from the side, configure a pattern to start searching from the side.

If two rescuers are available to conduct a signal search on a wide runout, they can start two straight or zigzag lines to provide necessary coverage within the search strip width recommended for their particular units. (See Figure 6-5.)

If multiple searchers are available to conduct the signal search on a wide runout, they should proceed in straight lines, side by side. This gives them greater speed and the ability to maintain more accurate distances between themselves.

The outside searchers may need to start a zigzag pattern to adequately cover debris if it gets wider toward the toe of the avalanche. (See Figure 6-6.)

Figure 6-7 shows rescuers entering from the side and starting their search there with one zigzagging upslope and the other downslope. In this case the LSA is well defined and close to the start of the debris, and the victim was last seen turning to their left. Because of this, the rescuers can concentrate their search on that side of the debris. If the LSA was less well defined, more in the middle or higher up from the start of the debris, the rescuers would widen their search pattern across the slope.

When a signal is acquired, announce, mark, and proceed to the coarse search. One or two rescuers can follow the signal while others prepare to probe and shovel. Depending upon how many people are buried and how many searchers there are, some searchers may continue to search for another signal.

Coarse search

This part of the search is dependent on the type of beacon being used. Most transceivers help the rescuer follow the flux lines generated by the transmitting beacon by using a digital display with distance and directional arrows or lights. When within about three meters, proceed to the fine search.

Figure 6-6. Signal search of wide runout with multiple searchers available

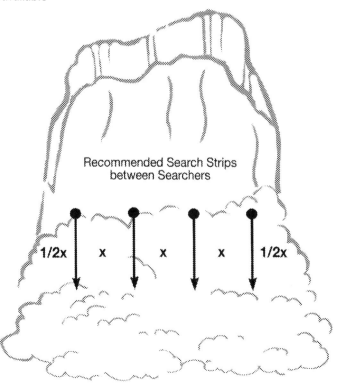

Recommended Search Strips between Searchers

1/2x   x   x   x   1/2x

Fine search

This is usually a small grid that brings the rescuer even closer to the buried transceiver. For best results, get the receiving beacon down near the snow surface, move slower, make straight lines, and mark fade points. Other rescuers can be getting probes and shovels ready.

Pinpoint search

Pinpoint the exact location by probing. Use a pattern for probing. Some suggested patterns include a spiral out from the first probe, a small grid, or concentric circles. A probe spacing of twenty-five centimeters (ten inches) will give about a 99% chance of a strike (see figure 6-8).

As with all finds, the leader must make decisions about reassigning rescuers. Considerations are based on shoveling needs, the number of other buried victims, and the number of rescuers, the size of the debris left to search, and any other pertinent information available. If other rescuers are continuing the transceiver search, they may need to form a new signal-search pattern given that there are fewer searchers.

At the conclusion of the transceiver search, make sure that all rescuers switch back to "transmit." Have rescuers raise their hand when they have switched to ensure that everyone has heard the command.

Figure 6-7. Signal search with two rescuers entering from the side of the debris

TIPS:

• In practice exercises, instead of doing only single rescuer beacon searches, occasionally practice organizing a group of people to search a large area.

• During the first phase of a multiple burial search, it is important for each rescuer to mark the spot where one first detects a signal. Searchers may converge onto the same signal and will need to know where to resume the search for another signal. This avoids leaving areas not searched.

• The average depth of burial is about 1.2 meters (four feet), which is considered a very deep burial for transceiver search practice. Be sure to practice finding transceivers at this depth.

Figure 6-8. Probing patterns for transceiver pinpoint

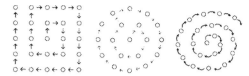

Spot probing

Spot probing is a rapid probing of likely catchment areas and around clues. When rescuers are first sent out on the debris to search for clues, they will also probe in likely areas that they encounter. Such areas may include irregularities on the snow surface and debris piled around rocks, trees, or at the bends and toe of the avalanche path.

A systematic probing pattern like a grid, a spiral, or concentric circles outward from the clue, tree, etc. should be used. (See Figure 6-8.)The probe spacing for spot probing can be increased to speed up the search. (In the pinpoint search with a transceiver, there is a small area to probe and a tighter probe spacing is appropriate.) For spot probing, a spacing of thirty centimeters (twelve inches) to fifty centimeters (twenty inches) gives the probability of detecting a buried person at 97% to 88% respectively. The probing should cover about two square meters. These are just guidelines and rescuers should make their own judgment depending on the size of the pile of debris and what they are trying to find. The entire toe of the debris is usually too large to spot probe but certainly any suspicious piles should be probed.

> **TIP:** Success may come quickly when a few rescuers join together briefly to create a mini two- to four-person probe line to probe a small, high-probability area. Then the rescuers can return to spot probing.

Perimeter search

The perimeter search is used to determine the edge of the debris and find tracks in and out of the slide. It may or may not be pertinent or practical for a particular situation. For a very large slide, it may be too difficult or too time consuming to get to these areas. However, if there is a possibility that the victim left the avalanche, a perimeter search could prove useful. Yellow flagging is the International Commission for Alpine Rescue (ICAR) standard for marking the perimeter.

Avalanche rescue dogs

A well-trained avalanche dog can be a great asset in a search operation, especially in the absence of transceivers. Avalanche dogs are growing in number in this country. Many ski areas have avalanche dogs on duty so they can respond to incidents in and near their boundaries. These are in addition to the search and rescue groups that include dog teams. Many handlers carry pagers, radios, and cell phones, and have arrangements with helicopters or other transportation to get into the field in a timely manner. If an area does not have a dog team, its preplan should specify those teams that are available and how to mobilize them. It is essential to realize that dogs can be successful in any phase of the operation.

Under good conditions, dogs can search an area much faster than a probe line. Patti Burnett, in her book, *Avalanche! Hasty Search: The Care and Training of Avalanche Search and Rescue Dogs,* describes what to consider when dog teams are deployed at an avalanche site. Some factors that affect a dog's search are duration of burial, wind, and air temperature. With respect to burial time, Burnett refers to Sandy Bryson's *Search Dog Training.* The scent diffusion rate will vary. In dry powder snow, the scent of a person buried one meter deep can reach the surface in a minute, while in wet snow, it may take fifteen minutes.

Cold temperatures are not a difficulty for dogs and actually allow the scent to rise through the snowpack more rapidly. The scent's diffusion rate depends on the temperature gradient between the victim and the snow surface, as well as the density of the debris. The depth of burial is another factor that determines the time it takes for scent to reach the surface. Hard slab chunks, rocks, streams and trees can channel the scent so that it does not necessarily surface directly above the buried person.

Wind is a key component in dog searching. Steady, low to moderate wind speeds are most beneficial for dogs. Strong, gusty winds make searching more difficult.

Dogs have sensitive noses, so whenever possible, try to position competing scents (including generators, snowcats, helicopters, snow machines, and other vehicles) away from the debris area or downwind.

Multiple dogs on scene can have a profound effect on the search. If the other dog(s) are not trained, they can interfere or distract the trained dogs, and should not be relied upon to "clear" an area. When working with other trained dog teams, it is important to coordinate strategy and efforts. It is also helpful to introduce the teams before they reach the deposition area.

Dog handlers should carry flags to mark alerts and these should be a color different from the already designated red, yellow, and blue. "DOG ALERT" should be written on the flag and it should be left in place for the duration of the search, whenever possible. The Site Leader should provide an Assistant to the dog handler to probe and shovel. Shoveling before attaining a probe strike is usually a waste of precious time and should be avoided unless the probe pole is shorter than the depth of the debris.

Dog teams should be well enough trained to work around other rescuers and

equipment. Burnett emphasizes that there is search and rescue dog etiquette. Rescuers must never call out to the dog while it is working, trying to get it to search an area or to play. The only person giving commands to the dog should be the handler.

In addition, searchers should not contaminate the slide area by urinating, throwing trash, or leaving their own equipment in undesignated locations. Never feed a rescue dog without express instructions from the handler. Never approach a rescue dog without permission.

> **TIP:** Rescuers should not sit on the debris because it has been shown that this added scent confuses rescue dogs.

If a rescue goes into multiple days, try to deploy dog teams prior to other rescuers' arrival. This gives the dogs a fresh, less contaminated area to work. Probed areas can have a Swiss-cheese effect, providing new paths for the scent to flow to the snow surface. Re-searching these areas may prove productive.

The Site Leader should consult with the Dog Team Leader about search strategy and coordination of operations. Dog Team Leaders need to know which areas have been searched, the location of clues that have been found, the LSAs, and the most likely burial sites.

Handlers should be able to report their confidence of negative results. The probability of detection (POD) is a number, usually a percent, indicating the handler's confidence that an area has been "cleared" given the current conditions. An example would be a POD of 70%, indicating that, with steady moderate winds, no distractions, effectiveness of the dog, etc., the handler is 70% confident that the area is "clear."

In the case of urban avalanche rescue, FEMA-certified urban search dogs may have an advantage over dogs trained specifically for alpine avalanche search and rescue. FEMA-trained dogs are familiarized with scents found in buildings and trained to alert only to human bodies, rather than clothing or other artifacts. They are trained to explore cavities and they work without wearing harnesses, which makes them less likely to be caught on wreckage and debris in tight spaces.

RECCO Avalanche Rescue System

Utilized by rescue teams since 1983, the RECCO system enables fast searching and directional pinpointing of a victim's precise location using harmonic radar. The two-part system consists of a handheld RECCO detector used by ski patrols and other organized rescue teams, and RECCO reflectors. These are small, passive electronic transponders that are integrated into apparel, helmets, protection gear, and boots. The reflector is permanently affixed, requires no training for use and needs no batteries to function. The reflector doubles the frequency and bounces back the directional radar signal, which is heard as a chirp-like signal. A RECCO reflector is not intended for companion rescue nor is it a substitute for a transceiver. All items that have RECCO reflectors are noted on hangtags and labels.

The latest detectors also incorporate an avalanche beacon receiver (457 MHz). This allows one rescuer to

perform both searches simultaneously. The RECCO detector is an additional tool for organized rescue teams that does not interfere with other rescue methods such as rescue dogs, transceiver searches, or probe lines. Today more than a thousand detectors are in place at six hundred resorts and with rescue teams around the world and these numbers continue to grow.

Some simple tips for using the RECCO detector:

- The detector operator should remove or reposition personal electronics (radios, cell phones, etc.). For example, a transceiver and radio should be

Figure 6-9. RECCO signal search

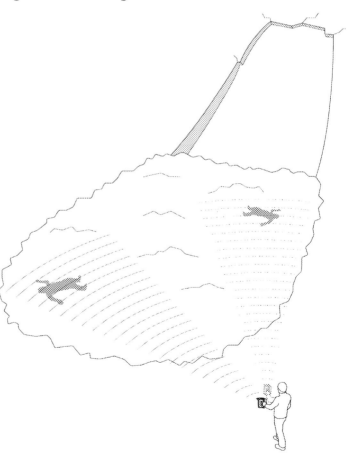

moved to the operator's back.
- Use the detector like a flashlight, as if searching at night.
- Turn your wrist slightly as you sweep the detector from side to side.
- Make at least two search passes.
- In wet snow, make the search corridors narrower and aim the detector more downward.

Signal search
- Scan debris from entry point before starting search pattern
- First pass: 20m wide search corridors, aim detector 4m ahead
- Second pass: 10m wide search corridors, aim detector 2m ahead

Coarse search (following signal)
- Mark spot where signal first detected
- Orient detector to strongest tone
- Follow signal

Fine search (getting close)
- Reduce power as needed
- Walk until tone disappears, should be above victim

Pinpoint search
- Hold detector vertically
- Turn wrist to optimize signal
- Reduce power
- Make rapid crisscross movements
- Mark spot with the strongest signal
- Probe to confirm spot and to determine depth

The RECCO detector can detect some electronic devices, like radios, electronic cameras, cell phones, GPS devices, and avalanche beacons, even when these devices are turned off. These devices are detected at much

shorter ranges than RECCO reflectors, but still offer another method of finding someone.

Like many electronic rescue devices, learning to use the RECCO detector is relatively easy; however, becoming proficient requires practice.

> **TIP:** When searching large debris areas, it's advantageous for a second rescuer to accompany each rescue-dog handler, transceiver searcher, or RECCO searcher. The second rescuer follows a few meters behind and marks the searcher's route and deals with radio communications. This allows the specialist to concentrate on his/her search, and enables other rescuers and leaders to quickly see what areas have been searched – and perhaps more importantly – what areas have not been searched.

Figure 6-10. RECCO coarse search

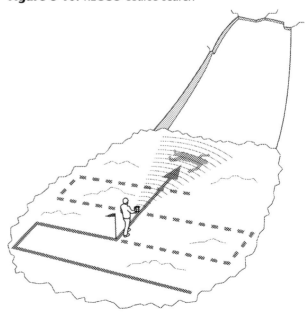

Figure 6-11. RECCO pinpoint search

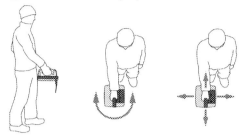

Probe lines

Formal probe lines are slow and concentrate many rescuers in a small area. Probe lines should be used judiciously and generally after other methods of search have been exhausted or when rescuers are plentiful. To maximize the chances of finding the victim alive, the Site Leader must identify, prioritize, and direct rescuers to start probing the highest probability areas. Using clues, witness statements, and any other available information, the leader can decide where to probe. Victims have been shoved under the apparently undisturbed snow at the toe of the debris, so probing should start or finish about a meter beyond the toe of the debris. Probing uphill is preferable because it's easier to control spacing.

The recommended probing technique is described in a paper from the 2006 International Snow Science Workshop, "Probing for avalanche victims revisited"

(see Selected References). This method uses a 50 x 50 centimeter grid spacing with each person probing three times per step forward. This gives an 88% chance of detecting the victim. (The previous spacing of 75 x 75 centimeter gave a 59% likelihood of detecting the victim). The 75 x 75 centimeter method using two probes per step can cover a given area much faster than the 50 x 50 centimeter spacing; however, the 75 x 75 centimeter method requires multiple passes more frequently and so the expected time until discovery is about the same. The real advantage of the 50 x 50 grid is generally finding the victim on the first pass.

Probing equipment and caches

In addition to the shovels and collapsible probes that most rescuers carry as personal gear, the rescue cache should contain non-collapsible probe poles of metal tubing of the same length, typically three to four meters. Longer poles are difficult to manage, and may deflect as they are pushed deeper into the debris. An advantage of standardizing probe lengths is that the Probe Line Leader may see when one probe is stopped short of full probe depth by an obstacle. The cache should also contain large metal shovels (grain scoops), red wands, and guide cords.

Guide cords are ropes with the probe

Figure 6-12. Distribution of probe holes compared with body profiles

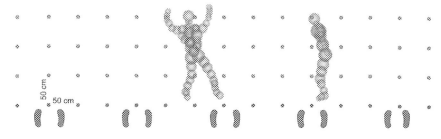

5 probers ≈ 7 meter search strip width

Figure 6-13. Sample section of a guide cord

interval marked as an aid for proper probe spacing. Cords can be marked using two colors: one color for the middle probe and another color for the left and right probe.

Probers center on the black flags and probe according to the directions given by the Probe Line Leader. Not only do guide cords ensure proper grid patterns, the cords also allow probe lines to move faster. Trials in Sweden by Peter Mågård demonstrated a 20% improvement in search speed. If no guide cord is available, probers can line up palm to palm. The leader should also have the probers set the probe fifty centimeters (about twenty inches) in front of them before stepping forward, to help visualize the correct distance.

Probe as deeply as possible without back strain. Burial statistics show that the chance of making a live rescue of a victim buried deeper than two meters is small. However, these statistics may be changing now that the use of AvaLungs can increase survival time and use of strategic shoveling can greatly speed up the recovery time of deeply buried people.

> **TIP:** A trick for using a guide cord in an area of trees or other obstacles is to split the cord in half and connect them back together with a small carabineer for easier movement around obstacles.

Probe line leadership

Before starting to probe avalanche debris, probers should be told the escape route. In the case of evacuation, the fleeing rescuers should leave the probes in place to mark the probe area and so they will not be encumbered.

Equipment:
- Six to ten rescuers with probes
- Shoveler(s) with shovels and spare probes
- Guide cord handlers with a guide cord and red marking wands

Responsibilities:
- Instruct untrained probers in probing technique
- Begin probe line where directed by the Site Leader
- Start with probers working uphill if possible
- Coordinate probing actions; three probes per step (e.g., left, center, right)
- Start slowly until proficiency develops
- The guide cord handlers can advance fifty centimeters as soon as the third probe is made
- Transition from voice to hand signals if possible
- Probes need to be inserted vertically
- Watch alignment, and height for consistency

Figure 6-14. Probe line alignment and spacing

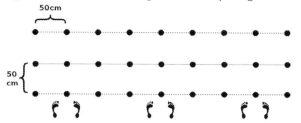

and vertically, which places the new probe holes between the first set. This produces more than a 99% probability of detection for the second pass. Without marking the first pass, offset is not possible, but the probability of detection is still better than 88%.

- Have handlers mark probe boundary every ten or so steps forward by placing a red wand at the probe hole on each end of the line

If a prober makes a strike:
- The prober announces, "Strike" and leaves the probe in place
- A shoveler gives a spare probe to the prober making the strike
- The probe line continues
- The shoveler confirms the strike with a spare probe and digs using strategic shoveling techniques described below
- The shoveler requests extra shoveling assistance if the strike indicates a deep burial

If a buried subject is confirmed, the shoveler(s) notify the Site Leader, who directs a Medical Team to assist.

Second pass
If a high-probability area is probed without detecting the buried victim, a second pass must be considered. If the area probed remains the most likely burial area based on all clues, it should be probed again before moving the probe line to another area. If a guide cord and flags are used to mark the first pass, the probe line can be offset by twenty-five centimeters horizontally

> **TIP:** How do you know you have a real strike? You want to eliminate as much unproductive shoveling time as you possibly can. If you get a spongy feel from the probe, it is most likely a person. If you are not sure, leave the first probe pole in place and use a second one to probe around the first to get an idea of the shape and feel of the object. If you hear a clinking sound, it may be a rock or ski, etc., so again probe around the first probe. You can also continue to probe as you dig.

Shoveling
Extricating a buried victim can be time consuming and hard work. In recent years, specific methods have evolved to save time and energy. In the case of companion rescue, when parties are

Figure 6-15. Alignment for second pass (dark dots represent first pass; white dots, second pass)

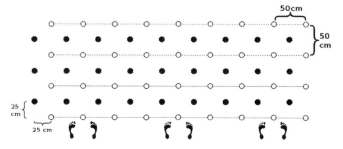

equipped with trans-ceivers, the shoveling phase is often the most time-consuming compo-nent of the rescue. Minutes saved can mean the difference between life and death.

Here are some general principles that will make digging easier and faster:

- Leave the probe pole in place. This confirms the exact location and depth of the victim.
- Dig obliquely from a short distance down-slope or to the side of the probe pole.
- Avoid standing over the buried victim to avoid collapsing the victim's air pocket.
- Lift snow as little as possible.
- Move snow only once.
- Keep your back straight.
- Use large muscle groups rather than arms alone.
- Wear gloves.
- Watch for an air pocket in front of face and nose.
- Create enough space to work on and care for the victim.

Strategic shoveling

This technique was developed specifi-cally for companion rescue when only one to four diggers are available.

- Leave the probe in place and move downslope of the victim approximate-ly one and a half times the burial depth.
- Dig a waist-deep starter hole about one "wingspan" (arms out to sides) wide.
- Dig downward and forward toward the probe. If two shovelers are avail-

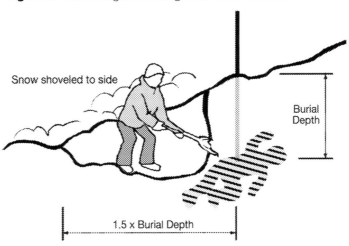

Figure 6-16. Strategic shoveling with one or two rescuers

Snow shoveled to side

Burial Depth

1.5 x Burial Depth

able, dig side by side, about one "wingspan" apart.
- Throw snow to sides.
- Move into starter hole when about waist deep and continue digging downward and forward. As depth increases, snow can be cleared to the back of the hole rather than lifted and tossed to the sides.
- Additional shovelers can clear snow downhill and work to create a plat-form upon which primary diggers can place snow.
- Use a scraping action to clear snow when getting close to the buried sub-ject.
- Use the first body part uncovered to estimate location of head.
- Use hands to clear the subject's face and airway; dig out chest.
- When the entire body is freed, extri-cate gently to platform and continue to perform necessary emergency care.

V-Shaped Conveyor Belt

Developed by Manuel Genswein of Switzerland, this method works especially well when many diggers are available.

- Begin digging down-slope of the subject as described above. On flat debris, the length of the "V" will be about twice the burial depth. On a steep slope, the length will be about equal to the burial depth.
- Arrange shovelers in a wedge-shaped or inverted "V" pattern.
- The lead shoveler at the apex chops snow into blocks and scoops snow downslope.
- Assisting shovelers use paddling-like motions to move snow further downslope, building up a wedge-shaped level platform.
- Shovelers rotate clockwise about every five minutes.
- Use a scraping action to clear snow when getting close to the buried subject. Additional shovelers may join lead shovelers to help clear snow and increase the working space.
- Use the first body part uncovered to estimate the location of the head.
- Use hands to clear the subject's face and airway; dig out chest.
- When the entire body is freed, extricate gently to platform; perform necessary emergency care.

Figure 6-17. Conveyor shoveling method using multiple shovelers

Helicopters

In the twenty-first century, helicopters have emerged as a critical tool in avalanche rescue. Helicopters – when weather conditions permit – provide rescuers with fast access to incident sites and speedy, smooth evacuations for the injured. Helicopters save time, effort and lives. Despite the benefits of using a helicopter, rescuers must remember that helicopters may increase rescuers' risk, so it is important that rescuers work with the pilot (and flight crew, if available).

In addition to transporting rescuers and victims, helicopters can search with a long-range beacon receiver and RECCO. The long-range beacon receiver is an external beacon antenna that is suspended beneath the helicopter. The RECCO operator holds the detector out the door. With both devices, it is important for the pilot to know how to use the device on the ground, as the pilot will fly a similar search pattern. The signal search patterns for both devices can be the same. When a beacon signal is heard the pilot flies in the direction of the strongest signal. With RECCO, the pilot follows the directional signal. When the pilot gets close, a marker is dropped from the helicopter. Then a field team finishes the search, or the pilot drops off rescuers.

Helicopter operations in mountain rescue involve extra risks and safety challenges because of the added dangers of off-airport landings and sometimes poor weather conditions. The process of reducing risks should start with pre-season meetings and trainings with the pilot and aircraft. In addition to these trainings, here are a few helicopter safety guidelines.

Helispots

Temporary landing zones, or LZs, are properly called helispots, which can be found along ridges and meadows. Pilots prefer not to take off or land vertically. Helicopters need room to maneuver and the ideal helispot is flat and about the size of a football field. If such space is not available, seek an area at least 100 x 100 feet in size that is free of obstacles and loose materials (snow and overhead wires). The pilot will land and take off into the wind. Place a well-secured, heavy backpack or wands at the upwind edge of the helispot to provide a fixed reference point for the pilot. Do not use a snowmobile as the windshield and other parts can blow off. Rescuers should expect significant blowing snow for several seconds when the helicopter lands and takes off.

Communications

As the helicopter approaches, establish radio communications with the pilot and give "clock" directions: twelve o'clock is straight in front of the helicopter, three o'clock is off the right door, six o'clock is the tail, and nine o'clock is the left door. Provide wind direction and speed, including gusts. Also alert the pilot to any potential hazards, like nearby power or lift lines, or soft and loose snow in the helispot.

Important dos and don'ts:

- All items worn by and carried by rescuers must be secure.
- Do not mark the helispot with anything that can blow around or be blown up into the blades.
- Only approach the helicopter after the pilot sees you and waves you in.
- Always approach from between the ten and two o'clock positions.
- Never approach or exit a helicopter uphill.
- Keep a crouching, low body position.
- Never walk around the back of a helicopter or approach from the rear.
- Never carry anything above your shoulders (drag skis with poles tied together).
- Never wear baseball-style or cowboy-type hats around a helicopter. Tight-fitting ski caps are OK. Wear goggles to protect your eyes.
- Keep dogs on leashes at all times.
- Never load equipment or secure doors and latches without a crew member's supervision.
- Waving arms from horizontal to crossed overhead means, "Do not land."

> **TIPS:**
> • The first team flying into an Incident Site should take some time to search the debris from the air. The helicopter provides a unique and efficient vantage point when searching for clues.
> • The first team should not leave the helicopter until radio communications have been established with the pilot. Initially the pilot may be the team's only link to the Incident Commander.

GPS

The Global Positioning System is a satellite navigation system developed by the U.S. Department of Defense. More than two dozen satellites transmit signals that allow GPS receivers to determine the user's location and travel speed. Already used by many people for navigation, GPS receivers can be helpful in avalanche rescue for recording the position of clues, tracking rescuers' search routes and probe lines. GPS can also be used to direct rescue helicopters to incidents and to direct rescuers back to the trailhead after getting a one-way helicopter flight to the Incident Site. Also, when bad weather threatens to chase rescuers from an Incident Site, GPS receivers can capture location coordinates of clues and the perimeter of the debris. These features can be accurately re-located when the weather improves and the search resumes.

> **TIP:** On very large avalanches, GPS can be used to track where searchers have and have not been.

• *Chapter Seven* •

Rescue Operations

Rescue operations are performed in basically the same manner for on-area and backcountry rescues, whether conducted by companions or by organized rescue teams. The decisions and variables involved are the same.

Immediate Search

In any avalanche rescue operation, variables present both solutions and problems for avalanche rescue leaders. The person in charge at the Incident Site must recognize the variables involved at the Incident Site and make decisions on how best to use the available personnel and equipment. In the face of the given hazards, he/she must establish where and how to start looking for the victims.

> **Variables in avalanche rescue:**
> • Personnel
> • Hazard
> • Weather
> • Clues
> • Equipment
> • Number of victims
> • Location
> • Access
> • Size
> • Time

The right mix of variables (e.g. an adequate number of trained and equipped personnel and favorable weather) may lead to a successful operation. Conversely, poor weather alone may shut down an operation, no matter how well trained and equipped the personnel. The use of transceivers, RECCO, and dogs, added to the number of clues found, improves the chances of success even if the avalanche is quite large. The lack of clues, even in a small slide, can prolong the rescue.

Immediate Search Team

The Immediate Search Team, typically three to seven people, is the first team to reach the Incident Site. The leader should be an experienced rescuer, because this person's decisions will affect the rest of the operation.

To get the Immediate Search Team to the Incident Site as quickly as possible, rescuers and their equipment should be in top condition. Team members' abilities to travel over snow should be similar. The more difficult the access to the Incident Site, the more important it is for rescuers' physical conditioning, abilities, and mode of travel to be similar.

A significant difference between the backcountry and developed-area rescue is the personal equipment carried by rescuers in the Immediate Search Team and other first responding field teams. When an incident happens in or near a developed area, there is usually little reason to take in personal bivouac gear. However, in the back-

Figure 7-1. Immediate search decision-making flow chart

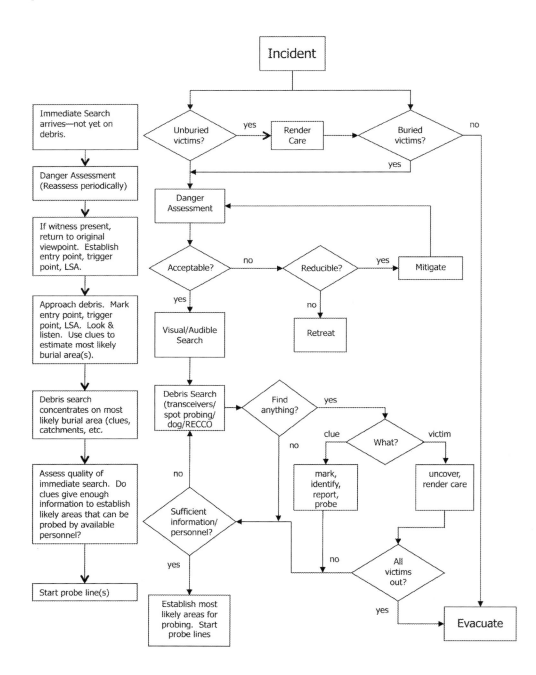

country, rescuers should always carry adequate personal bivouac gear. Weather or mechanical problems may ground the helicopter, and technical terrain, equipment problems, or an injured rescuer may keep support teams from reaching the Incident Site. Having bivouac gear allows rescuers to take care of themselves and the victim(s) until medical and evacuation equipment can reach the Incident Site.

As the first responding team, this group is responsible for determining a safe route into the Incident Site, marking the route, and relaying this information to the Incident Commander (IC). In the best-case scenario, the rescue plan lists potentially safe routes and the route to the Incident Site is determined before the team sets out, but the Immediate Search Team must confirm the actual safety of the route.

The Immediate Search flow chart

This decision-making flow chart (Figure 7-1) aids in helping to make the type of decisions necessary at the Incident Site. For detailed descriptions of search techniques and technologies, see Chapter 6.

Every mountain rescue situation is different and requires flexibility of the Immediate Search Team Leader and rescuers to adapt the model so the victim(s) can be found in the shortest possible time without placing the victim(s) and rescuers at additional risk.

Once at the Incident Site, the Immediate Search Team Leader is faced with a series of decisions concerning the safety and success of the operation. If survivors are present, the Immediate Search Team must check them first; it may only take a few seconds to assess their condition. They may be uninjured and able to assist in searching. If a survivor is injured, cold, weak, or a potential liability, at least one rescuer must give care to him/her while

the others continue searching for the buried victim(s).

Witnesses

Interviewing all witnesses will greatly aid in the search effort. (See Appendix, Sample Witness Interview Sheet.) Search and rescue managers should make every effort to get the witness back to the Incident Site. If possible, take the witness to where he/she was when the avalanche occurred to get the best perspective for estimating last seen areas (LSAs). The witness can help identify clues at the scene, which will aid in establishing a trajectory for a given victim and distinguishing one victim's clues from another. Someone should be assigned to stay with the witness.

Often in backcountry avalanche search and rescue, it is not possible or feasible to have the witness accompany the Immediate Search Team. The witness may be too tired and thus will slow the Immediate Search Team in reaching the Incident Site.

Danger assessment

The fact that a life is in jeopardy does not justify jeopardizing more lives.

The team conducts a danger assessment of the Incident Site before going onto the debris. The fact that one avalanche has occurred strongly suggests instability on similar slopes in the vicinity. Obvious dangers that may keep rescuers out of an area include deteriorating weather, darkness, or the potential for another avalanche. The team should determine whether wind and new snow have reloaded the starting zone of the old slide, if there are other avalanche-starting zones that funnel into the same debris area, or if there is hangfire (snow above the fracture line that has not yet released but could). Remember, assessment of hazards is an ongoing process that continues throughout the entire operation.

One thing is clear: If a significant avalanche hazard exists, something must be done to mitigate the danger. The potential need for mitigation should be addressed in the written rescue plan and arranged previously with the local ski patrol, Forest Service, highway department, or county sheriff's department. If the rescuers cannot mitigate the danger, they should retreat.

Older rescue plans may mention the action of posting an avalanche guard. Rarely can an avalanche guard be effective. Even slow avalanches travel faster than rescuers can run, especially over avalanche debris. Further, posting a guard could significantly decrease the searching efficiency by decreasing the number of searchers available. In any case, emergency escape routes, a warning signal and a meeting place should be established for rescuers. If sufficient personnel are available, avalanche guides can guide rescuers to the Incident Site and keep non-rescuers out of the area. Spotters can watch rescue crews, especially in urban and highway incidents. (See Chapter 8.)

Approach search

As the team approaches the debris, it performs a visual search for clues (victims, clothing, equipment, tracks, and flow of the avalanche). The team periodically calls out the victims' names and listens for a response.

If no one witnessed the slide and there are tracks going into the slide, rescuers should look for an equal number of tracks exiting the slide. It is also a good idea to examine the tracks to make sure they were not made by an animal, such as an unlucky elk or mountain goat.

Debris search

Once on the debris, the team continues to search visually and audibly. Team member are given assignments, areas to search, and directions for what to do when they have completed their tasks. Assignments will be based on what is seen on the approach and all other information available. Unless it is certain that no victims were wearing transceivers, rescuers should conduct a transceiver search.

Rescuers not involved in the transceiver search can start marking LSAs and tracks (if this is practical), and begin spot probing likely catchment areas. A perimeter search should be conducted (if possible) on the off chance that the victim escaped or the victim or clues were thrown beyond the debris area. Rescuers should try to establish the victim's trajectory or flow line as he/she was carried down in the slide. Clues that are found help establish likely burial areas. Likely burial areas should be spot probed: around rocks and trees, lumps, depressions, and the inside and outside edges of bends. It is also a good practice to continue to call out and listen. A clue such as a ski pole or ski should be checked to see if it is still attached to a victim. All clues should be marked with blue flags and left in place. Rescuers must quickly and systematically spot probe around the clue. Each clue should be identified, if possible, by consulting any witnesses, or witness information, to determine its owner. The flagged ski or pole is stood upright; a flagged mitten or hat can be attached to a wand or branch. Document and report all clues to your leader. People found are cared for immediately.

Initiate searches by rescue dogs and RECCO as soon as they are available at the Incident Site. Both of these teams can work while other rescue efforts are in progress.

Before starting a probe line that will dramatically slow the speed of the search, the quality of the Immediate Search must be assessed. The important question to ask is, "Do the clues give a sufficient amount of information to establish the likely burial areas that can be probed with available personnel?" If the answer is no, return to the debris search phase and look for additional information. How long should this take? At the Peak 7 incident near Breckenridge, Colorado in February 1987, the deposition covered an area the size of almost thirty football fields. In less than twenty minutes, fewer than a dozen ski patrollers completed the Immediate Search. The rescuers gathered enough clues to confine searching to an area half that size. A smaller slide may take much longer to search, if no clues are found immediately or there are many catchment areas to investigate.

Sometimes even after repeating the debris search a time or two, no equipment or clothing will be found, and the only clues for likely burial spots are tracks or LSA(s). It is not a lot of information to start with, but it must be sufficient. Once rescuers have obtained the maximum information, and high-priority search areas have been identified, the probe lines can begin.

> **TIP:** When there are few rescuers available to search, the Immediate Search Team Leader can participate in the searching. However, the leader must keep an eye on the entire effort at the same time. This will be difficult and so the leader should remove him or herself from active searching and concentrate on directing the search effort as soon as enough personnel arrive at the site.

Immediate Search leadership

As previously mentioned, the initial actions of the Immediate Search Leader critically affect the safety of rescuers and the final outcome of the operation.

Here is a partial list of the Immediate Search Leader's responsibilities:

Assemble personnel and equipment
- Select three to seven team members
- Include witness(es) if possible
- Include avalanche dog and handler and RECCO, if immediately available
- Provide shovels, transceivers and probes for each member
- Provide extra probes and shovels
- Provide first aid gear
- Provide flagging wands per the International Commission for Alpine Rescue (ICAR)
- Mark the safe route in (any color not blue, red or yellow):
  - Blue – clues
  - Red – probed areas
  - Yellow – debris perimeter
- Assess avalanche danger between departure point and Incident Site
- Plan appropriate route for safety and speed
- Organize transportation (self, snow machines, helicopter, etc.)
- Consider the need for avalanche mitigation measures
- Brief team members
- Perform transceiver check

Notify Incident Dispatcher when ready
- Do not depart without Incident Dispatcher clearance
- Leave roster of personnel and equipment at Staging Area (departure point)

Travel to Incident Site
- Use quickest safe route
- Flag route for following teams
- Alert IC if route is not suitable for the transport of medical and evacuation gear

Upon arrival at Incident Site
- Assume role of Site Leader until relieved
- Assess if safe to search
- If not, mitigate or call in control team

If a companion search is underway:
- assess status
- take charge

Commence Immediate Search
- Conduct quick visual/auditory search (look, shout, listen)
- Designate Incident Site Staging Areas for rescuers' personal equipment
- Set emergency escape plan, designate signal and safe meeting place
- Sketch the Incident Site, use a digital camera and update as search proceeds
- Assign jobs and areas to be searched
- Mark last seen area(s) (LSAs), clues, tracks in and tracks out, if possible
  - Indicate LSA by two crossed blue flags
- Search debris surface below LSA
  - Check, mark and identify to whom clue(s) belong
  - Leave clue(s) in place
- Conduct transceiver / RECCO / dog searches
- Spot probe high-probability areas
- Do a perimeter search and mark with yellow flags if warranted or possible
- Reevaluate after each clue or victim is found

Extended Responsibilities
- Integrate additional resources as they arrive
- Brief, identify caches, show escape route(s) and inform about the signal
- Identify leaders and assign tasks
- Start formal probe line when:
  - enough information is available to establish high-probability area(s)
  - enough equipment/personnel are available
- Maintain site cleanliness
- Maintain contact with IC or designated leader
- Maintain leadership at the site until relieved or reassigned

The Immediate Search Leader must anticipate the necessary changes in priorities of the rescue effort when a victim is found during the immediate search. In the case of a single victim, the search actions immediately shift to providing medical care and evacuation. If there are multiple victims, the leader must anticipate the numbers of rescuers needed to manage the extrication and care for one victim, while continuing the search effort for others. With many rescuers, the situation can be easily handled. When rescuers are few, attention may have to be focused on the first victim found.

Continuing search operations

When the designated Site Leader arrives at the Incident Site, a crucial exchange of information is needed with the Immediate Search Leader. The Site Leader needs to know the progress of the search, the people found and their condition, other leaders at the site and their tasks, what clues have been found, condition of the rescuers, and what resources are anticipated. A sketch of the Incident Site by the Immediate Search Leader greatly contributes to the sharing of information. It is strongly recommended that the Site Leader designate the Immediate Search Leader as an Assistant. This arrangement creates a strong management team.

> **TIP:** Having the Site Leader wear a bright-colored vest makes it easier to identify this person in the field.

Site leadership
Site Leader responsibilities:
- Meet with Immediate Search Team Leader and transfer command
- Reassign Immediate Search Team Leader as an Assistant (recommended)
- Incorporate arriving rescuers into the operation

- As the size and complexity of the operation increases, appoint leaders, managers and assistants as needed
- Reevaluate the overall operation:
  - with each clue or subject found
  - with any change in conditions (e.g., deteriorating weather)
- Anticipate and request additional support
- Appraise IC of significant events during the operation (such as subjects found, condition)
- Determine need for extra medical support, transportation/evacuation
- Gauge increasing avalanche hazard at site
- Consult with Safety Assistant, if position filled
- Maintain/establish emergency escape plan, danger warning signal, and safe meeting place
- Confirm/Designate an equipment and personnel Staging Area
- Appoint an Incident Site Staging Manager to meet and instruct arriving rescue teams
- Confirm/Designate a medical Staging Area and coordinate with Medical/ Evacuation Teams
- Designate/mark a helispot
- Establish support area for rescuers
  - Water/food
  - Shelter/heater
  - Latrine
  - Supplemental gear, blankets, clothing (esp. gloves), probes, shovels, etc.
  - Arrange for rescuer relief/rotation
  - Arrange for all personnel and equipment to safely return from the Incident Site

TIP: Use the NSP *Avalanche Rescue Quick Guide* as a field reference for leadership checklists and search techniques or make your own checklists.

Tracking search operations

About one quarter of serious avalanche incidents (those that have killed or injured people) are wider than 168 meters (550 feet). When an avalanche debris area is quite large (one or two football fields or larger), tracking the searched and unsearched areas can become quite confusing.

Some strategies to deal with this situation include:
- dividing the avalanche debris into geographical Divisions and assign Division Supervisors.
- roping off or flagging sectors or regions and assigning a leader to each area.

Keep careful track of areas that have been searched but, more importantly, what has not been searched. Most avalanche rescue practice areas tend to be very small compared to actual avalanche debris areas so tracking the operation rarely gets practiced. Try to set up some practices that use larger areas.

Example of a rescue unfolding over time

In the following Figures, black flags represent red for probed and searched areas, gray flags represent blue for clues and LSAs, and white flags represent yellow for marking the avalanche perimeter.

Figure 7-2 shows an example of the Immediate Search Team's actions upon arriving to an Incident Site with two buried victims. Clues are the tracks into the slide. Clues also come from witnesses who have approximate locations of the last seen areas (LSAs). The team has assessed the risks and deemed them acceptable to search the slide. Escape routes are identified and told to all. The team has also established the Incident Site Staging Area where they left behind their skis.

The Immediate Search Team has started

Figure 7-2. Immediate search

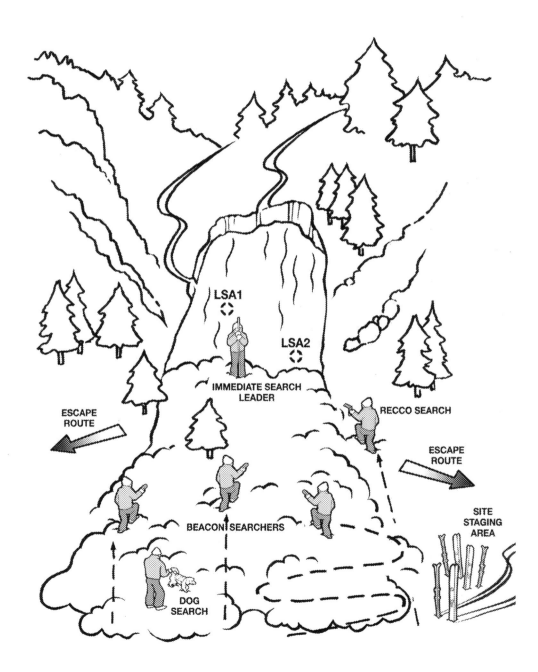

Figure 7-3. Expanded immediate search

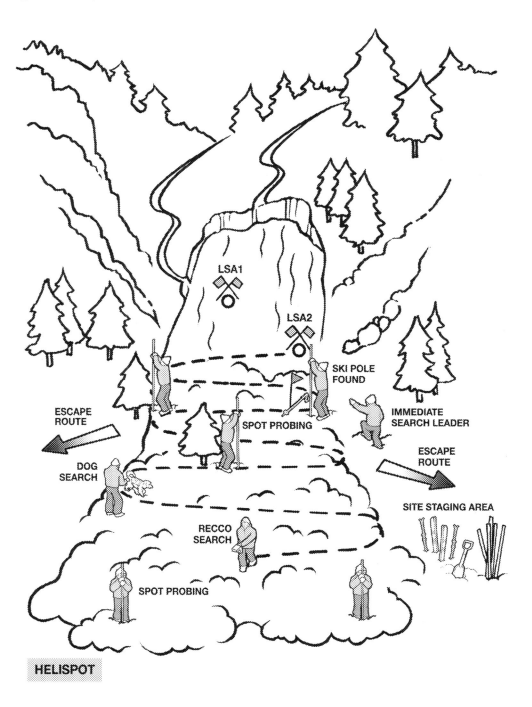

Figure 7-4. Full search

LSA1

LSA2

DOG
SEARCH

ESCAPE
ROUTE

SITE LEADER

ASSISTANT

ESCAPE
ROUTE

SITE STAGING AREA

SPOT
PROBING

MANAGER

MEDICAL TEAM

HELISPOT

the transceiver search, dog search and RECCO search. The team arrived from the bottom of the slide and is working upslope. At this point, with relatively few rescuers, the Immediate Search Team Leader is actively participating in the search. Additional rescuers are headed to the Incident Site.

In Figure 7-3, additional rescuers have arrived. The transceiver search is complete and found no signals. The LSAs have been marked with crossed blue flags. Rescuers have found a ski pole belonging to Skier 2. Spot probing is occurring around the clue and other likely areas. The Immediate Search Team Leader has moved to a better vantage point to manage and direct the search effort. At this point, he/she will likely have appointed subordinate leaders to help manage rescuers on the debris because of the increasing number of rescuers working over a large area.

In Figure 7-4, the search effort is well underway. The Incident Site Staging Manager receives and briefs arriving groups of rescuers. A probe line has started at the toe to search in line with clues for Skier 2. Red flags mark the probed area. The dog search continues while other rescuers spot probe likely areas and look for clues for Skier 1. The Site Leader has arrived and is assisted by the Immediate Search Team Leader. The debris perimeter has been marked with yellow-colored flags.

These Figures show how a rescue might evolve, but remember that rescue is a creative process. Each rescue is unique, and there are many ways to organize people and equipment. Practice and experience will be your best guide in managing a rescue as it grows and changes in complexity and size, and also as the operation winds down.

• *Chapter Eight* •

Different Settings for Avalanche Rescue

The general goals of avalanche rescue – to find, to treat, to evacuate the buried avalanche victim, and to manage the operation safely – never change even though the settings are often different. However, different settings can make big differences in the methods used to accomplish those goals.

Well-prepared ski patrols and rescue teams plan and train for avalanche incidents that occur in six basic settings:

1) Resort
2) Side/Slack Country
3) Front Country
4) Backcountry
5) Highway
6) Urban

To operate effectively in different settings requires well-thought-out rescue plans that are shared and practiced between rescue agencies. Having one or two face-to-face meetings between all rescue leaders each fall will greatly improve the interaction and coordination of rescues.

Rescuers should recognize that despite their unchanging goals, the different settings and circumstances of each rescue operation might result in unique challenges and dangers. Adding to these difficulties is the possibility of combined settings for which rescuers and rescue organizations must be ready.

For example, ski patrollers train long and hard to rescue a buried rider, but are they aware of the challenges and ready if a building, like a restaurant within the resort, is struck? How about the mountain rescuer who encounters an avalanche-blocked road while driving over a mountain pass or firefighters who respond to the call of a buried child caught sledding in a ravine at the edge of town?

These situations require different skills and the knowledge of different experts and organizations working together. It means bringing together organizations that have not worked together, e.g. avalanche rescuers working with urban search and rescue teams, firefighters, highway workers or railway workers. Ski patrollers know avalanche rescue, but may not know how to work in and around damaged buildings. Likewise, the urban rescuer or firefighter is trained to work in and around collapsed structures but probably has little or no experience in avalanche rescue.

The following are some of the special problems, challenges and dangers rescuers face. When reading these descriptions, it is important to realize that every incident can be just as dissimilar as they might be similar. It is not uncommon for avalanche incidents to occur in the same general spot; however, if on one day a helicopter is used to transport rescuers into the Incident Site and the victim(s) out, operational and logistical decisions may be very different than on a day without the helicopter.

Ways to improve how different agencies work together are introduced in Chapter 5.

Resort (on-area) rescue

Organized avalanche rescue was developed to handle primarily the problems of avalanche incidents within ski areas.

Some special challenges of on-area rescue include:

- many skiers and riders on site before ski patrollers arrive
- confusion and uncertainty as to who may be caught
- confusion because of significant numbers of people at the Incident Site
- the need to operate the rest of the resort concurrent with the incident response
- the involvement of multiple on-mountain departments and off-mountain agencies
- the presence of news reporters

Planning strategies
- Identify potential problem areas
- Identify resources
- Develop and practice a rescue plan
- Include other on-mountain departments in training and practice

Rescue strategies
- Close nearby lifts to guests
- Use guides to keep non-rescuers out and to screen volunteers
- Have several rescuers available to interview witnesses
- Ensure that transceiver, RECCO and dog searches are thoroughly done
- Designate someone to manage guests and volunteer rescuers
- Be sure leaders are authoritative and easy to spot
- Consider dividing large search areas into Divisions
- Carefully track and mark sectors that have been searched, and that still need to be searched

- Use radio frequency identification (RFID) scanners to track volunteers and to identify possible missing persons
- Search parking lots and local hotels if necessary to locate missing persons
- When a victim is found, keep others searching unless the number of people missing is certain

Special problems challenge ski patrollers when avalanches hit buildings, parking lots or access roads. Please see the Highway and Urban sections on pages 64 and 65.

> **TIP:** Include non-rescue skiers in drills to practice managing and using untrained volunteers.

Side/Slack country (off-area) rescue

Many avalanche incidents occur in side- or slack-country terrain adjacent to or near ski resorts. Whether accessed from backcountry gates along the ski area boundary or skiers or riders "ducking" under ropes, rescues in the side/slack country combine the challenges of both resort and backcountry rescues, including:

- potential confusion from numerous calls by different witnesses to 911 operators
- potentially numerous untrained people at Incident Site, who may inadvertently obscure or move clues, obscure perimeters or contaminate the Incident Site before trained rescue teams arrive
- the arrival of individuals and organized rescue teams from different directions to multiple places along the avalanche
- the response by multiple rescue and supporting agencies, which can increase communications problems
- usually easy access but difficult egress
- ski patrollers who may be under-equipped for a prolonged effort outside the resort.

- bad weather or darkness that can make the side/slack country more like the backcountry
- rescue coordination between resort, local search and rescue, and law enforcement that changes the longer the operation goes
- potential workers' compensation/liability issues for ski patrollers and other ski area employees responding outside their resort

A rescue response to the side/slack country may seem simple and straightforward but rescuers can quickly discover all the challenges of a remote backcountry rescue that is located just a short distance from a resort. In addition to the strategies used in resorts, the following additional strategies may help in the side country.

Planning strategies
- Know the surrounding terrain and landmarks
- Keep current on snow conditions due to different aspects and elevations
- Have maps of the area
- Learn the locals' informal names for the terrain
- If allowed, visit potential problem areas

Rescue strategies
- Use guides to keep non-rescuers out and to direct rescuers in.
- Station rescuer(s) to contact skiers at return points back into the area to determine:
  - if they are witnesses
  - if they are people who have been reported missing

Front country rescue

Front country is terrain that borders urban areas and where the primary rescue agency is often the local fire department.

Rather than skiers and snowboarders, the users of the front country are likely to be snowshoers, trail runners, and kids sledding. Front country response involves elements of side country and backcountry responses but with urban rescue management. Features include:
- easy access and egress
- easy-to-ignore dangers because of easy access
- untrained individuals including friends and family immediately at Incident Site
- non-avalanche trained rescuers, who may arrive quickly
- news reporters who may arrive before rescuers
- rescue leaders who may not have avalanche rescue experience
- initial rescuers who may be unprepared for conditions or for a prolonged effort
- multiple agencies that will likely respond
- communication problems that increase as the number of agencies increases

Planning strategies
- Know which agency is responsible for search and rescue (fire, police, sheriff, Forest Service, etc.)
- Define ski patrol or mountain rescue's role in response
- Plan for crowd and traffic control
- Use a Public Information Officer from the lead agency to work with news reporters

Rescue strategies
- Same as for side/slack country

Backcountry rescue

Most avalanche incidents occur in the backcountry where terrain and distances often impede response time. Cell phones, snowmobiles, and helicopters are reducing those times. Decisions made by rescuers tend to have greater consequences in a remote setting.

Significant challenges include:
- greater distances between Command Post and Incident Site
- difficulty finding the incident
- difficult or long access and egress between trailhead and Incident Site
- difficult or long access to the trailhead
- possible multiple modes of transportation used (aircraft, mechanized and non-mechanized surface travel) that can complicate coordination of arrival times at Incident Site
- skiers and snowshoers in the same team traveling at different speeds, increasing the risk of team separation
- multiple agencies that will likely respond
- communication problems that arise as more agencies are involved and as distances increase
- unforeseen situations that are more likely to arise
- mitigation of adjacent avalanche dangers that are difficult or impossible
- the wrong attitude held by many rescuers that backcountry rescues are only body recoveries

Planning strategies
- Know the surrounding terrain, including landmarks and GPS coordinates
- Keep current on snow conditions at different aspects and elevations
- Have maps of the area
- Learn the locals' informal names for the terrain
- Pre-plan for explosive mitigation
- Identify different sources/modes of transportation that could be made available if an incident occurs
- Have backup plans for when situations do not go as expected
- Planning ahead for multi-day operations becomes more critical

Rescue strategies
- Carefully screen who should respond into the field. Consider:
  - physical fitness
  - personal gear
  - mode of travel
- Group rescuers by their mode of travel
- Provide rescuers with radios, maps, and GPS coordinates
- Anticipate and be proactive about:
  - communications, including radio relays, ham radios, satellite phones, etc.
  - Staging Areas, including Command Post and Incident Site

While mountain rescue teams and ski patrols have trained for years to work effectively in the backcountry, some important changes have occurred in how operations are managed. Perhaps the biggest change from years ago is the response of multiple agencies that must work together to perform a rescue.

Highway rescue

Transportation departments around the country do a tremendous job keeping roads open and safe. However, with increased traffic, the possibility of avalanche incidents increases.

Avalanche incidents along highways often present unique challenges to rescuers accustomed to working in resorts or in the backcountry.
- Incidents almost always involve a natural avalanche
- Incidents usually involve a greater threat of additional avalanches
- It's difficult to know who or how many victims are trapped
- Many untrained individuals are immediately at the Incident Site
- There are crowd and traffic problems due to the proximity of adjacent paths
- Traffic volume needs to be managed, including getting unaffected vehicles

moved away from potential avalanche runout zones
- Incidents may occur at night
- Victim(s) may or may not be inside vehicles
- Victim(s) and others at the scene may not be dressed for winter conditions
- Organized rescue team(s) may not be able to reach the site because of traffic congestion or other avalanches
- Rescue response can arrive from two directions
- Typical metal detectors will probably not locate a buried vehicle
- Survival time may be stretched to many hours if victim(s) are protected by vehicle

Planning strategies
- Gather information before the event:
  - highway avalanche atlas
  - likely problem spots, e.g., frequent running avalanche paths or paths with runout zones ending in ravines or water (rivers, lakes or sea)
  - avalanche-paths histories
  - safe spots along the road for staging and parking
  - spots with good radio/cell phone communications
- Develop and practice a rescue plan
- Develop and update a resource list each fall
- Motorists in avalanche terrain should consider carrying avalanche transceivers, probes, shovels, warm clothing, etc.
- Highway workers should develop a work plan that spells out how to operate in avalanche terrain including using spotters and working in pairs. Workers should have basic avalanche safety and rescue training and rescue equipment

Rescue strategies
- Close road with manned checkpoints to limit unnecessary traffic
- Assess the dangers at the Incident Site and on adjacent slopes
- Turn waiting traffic around and move vehicles and people to safe areas
- Coordinate with rescuers or motorists on the other side of the avalanche
- Determine if it's safe to search
- Use a spotter/guard
- For a buried vehicle, try using a magnetometer, a magnetic gradiometer, a ground penetrating radar or a RECCO detector
- If probing for a vehicle, use a larger grid pattern (1.2 by 1.2 meters, four by four feet)
- Stabilization of a vehicle with cribbing or anchoring may be necessary before attempting to remove passengers
- Vehicle extrication with special tools may be necessary to remove the vehicle from around the passenger

> **TIP:** Have small shovels or spades to clear snow from the vehicle's interior.

Urban rescue

Avalanche incidents involving structures, whether a single mountain cabin, a resort lodge, or an entire neighborhood pose special problems that may require a joint, interdisciplinary response by specialists. A ski patrol or mountain rescue team knows avalanche search and rescue, and a fire department knows urban search and rescue. To be successful in an urban avalanche rescue, effective leaders are needed to bring both organizations and other specialists together (structural engineers, utility workers, etc.).

Special considerations include:
- difficulty knowing who or how many are trapped

- the potential for a mass casualty incident
- victims who may or may not be within structures
- victims who may not be dressed for winter conditions
- difficulty knowing the precise location where houses and buildings were originally located
- many untrained volunteers immediately at the Incident Site
- many family members and friends at the Incident Site
- psychological concerns are very real for victims, families, and rescuers
- the threat of additional avalanches
- incidents occurring at night
- the high possibility of bad weather
- additional hazards from downed electrical lines, ruptured gas and water lines, voids (hollow areas), weakened structures and lots of invisible broken glass
- probing that's impeded by building rubble
- the need for specialized equipment
- alpine avalanche rescue dogs that may be distracted by food scraps and other unfamiliar scents (see Chapter 6, Avalanche rescue dogs)
- scents may channel long distances from victims
- organized rescue team(s) may have lost equipment in the avalanche
- rescuers may arrive from multiple directions
- survival time may be stretched to many hours or even days if victim(s) are protected by structures

Fortunately, urban avalanche rescue in the U.S. is uncommon, but as more people encroach into the mountains, surely these sorts of rescues will increase. Some important lessons have been learned, based on experiences of several very large urban avalanche rescues in Iceland and Europe in the 1990s.

Below are some general search strategies to help rescuers involved in an urban avalanche rescue.

Planning strategies
- Gather information before the event such as zoning maps, and GPS coordinates of landmarks, buildings, homes, street intersections, etc.
  - aerial photos/Google Earth images
  - type of construction
  - avalanche history
- Develop and practice a rescue plan
- Develop and update resource lists each fall:
  - arrange for specialized equipment including heavy excavation equipment, loaders, backhoes, sawzalls, pry bars, chain saws, tow chains, generators, lighting, etc.
  - investigate the availability of search dog teams trained to FEMA urban search dog standards
  - stage avalanche rescue equipment in multiple locations

> **TIP:** A team of six to eight shovelers and a small Medical Team (or specialist) should accompany each rescue dog.

Rescue strategies
- Assess dangers at Incident Site and on adjacent slopes
- Have backup rescuers available at all times, if additional avalanches are possible
- Have a scheme to find the original search area and clues in case heavy snow or a second avalanche covers the area
- Determine the debris area:
  - divide large search areas into sectors
  - estimate the orientation of the avalanche center and sides
- On the debris, locate and mark the locations of structures

- Consider time of day and the day of the week when considering where people were when the avalanche struck
- Determine buildings with the most potential for live finds
- Stabilize structures with cribbing and shoring when necessary before entering
- Search for victims by starting at the sides and working toward the center
- Search for and identify clues including:
  - wall colors
  - tiles
  - photo albums
  - addressed envelopes
- Locate, mark, and gather victims' personal belongings to return to relatives
- Look for voids (probe poles are better for finding voids than people)
- Shovel snow by hand to search
- Use heavy equipment to remove hand-shoveled snow

- Work short shifts of two to three hours
- Do not mix shoveled snow with unshoveled snow
- Mark searched snow with flagging or colored chalk
- Remember, some victims survive for many days in buried rubble

In slower moving avalanches, people tend to be in the rubble of buildings and homes, but victims of faster moving avalanches tend to be blown out into plain snow.

> **TIP:** In all rescue operations, it is important to provide the news media with good and timely information because witnesses or others may also tell the story over the Internet.

• Chapter Nine •

Medical Emergency Considerations

Burial in an avalanche is a medical emergency, and even when no one is buried, an avalanche can cause various sorts of medical emergencies. Asphyxia, trauma and hypothermia have always been associated with avalanche incidents and with mortality.

Asphyxiation is the most common cause of death. Three physiological processes conspire against the victim: hypoxia, hypercapnia, and hypothermia, the so-called Triple H Syndrome. For the buried victim, trauma worsens the Triple H Syndrome. Even for the unburied victim, traumatic injuries and hypothermia can be life threatening.

Asphyxia leads to hypoxia, or inadequate oxygenation of the body's tissues. Hypercapnia is the buildup of excess carbon dioxide caused by the re-breathing of exhaled air. Without a source of free air, hypercapnia leads to hyperventilation, unconsciousness and death.

Hypothermia is a drop in the body's temperature that affects almost all buried victims and many injured victims. Hypoxia and hypercapnia accelerates hypothermia, which in turn exacerbates the effects of hypoxia and hypercapnia – a vicious cycle. The best remedy for hypercapnia is a quick uncovering of the buried victim. One device that aids the buried victim against hypercapnia is the AvaLung™, which provides an open airway, an artificial air pocket, and a diverter that reduces the re-breathing of exhaled carbon dioxide.

While the consequences of asphyxiation are well known, recent reviews of incident case reports and medical records reveal that traumatic injuries are relatively common and hypothermia is almost certain. Avalanches associated with terrain traps, especially trees, cliffs and rock bands, contribute to a high rate of trauma. Ice climbers, often climbing in narrow gullies, and skiers and snowboarders skiing and riding in trees suffer the most trauma while snowmobilers – usually riding on open slopes – suffer little trauma. Avalanche victims often travel headfirst so head and thoracic injuries are common. Recently, researchers have started to recommend wearing helmets in avalanche terrain. Avalanche airbags are being redesigned to help protect the head, neck and chest.

Knowing the activity of the victim and sizing up the scene will provide clues about possible types of medical emergencies rescuers may encounter. Immediate transport to a higher level of care is critical for most buried victims.

It is beyond the scope of this book to discuss emergency care. However, the following common emergencies and basic treatment strategies are presented here so that rescuers can prepare for some of the most common emergencies. More specific treatment techniques can be found in the National Ski Patrol's *Outdoor Emergency Care* manual, and specific treatment protocols can be learned from the International Commission for Alpine Rescue (ICAR).

Asphyxia

In North America, asphyxiation causes about 75% of deaths for buried avalanche victims. Time is the enemy of the buried victim, but some buried victims do survive for many hours under the snow. Several U.S. avalanche victims have survived burials longer than twenty hours. Never give up on a rescue effort just because several hours have passed.

Mechanisms of asphyxia are:
- an obstructed airway caused by snow filling the air passages or from trauma to the face and neck
- compression of the chest interfering with respiratory movements
- hypercapnia caused by the build up of carbon dioxide in the air trapped around the head
- insufficient oxygen supply, particularly severe when the victim creates an ice mask by exhaling warm, moist air

To treat asphyxia:
- excavate the head and chest first
- look for the presence of an air pocket and a clear airway (important information for subsequent Advanced Life Support care)
- clear the air passages and make room for chest expansion
- open the airway (immobilize the spinal column if spinal, head or facial injury is suspected)
- assist ventilation if indicated (this can begin as soon as the head and chest are uncovered)

Trauma

In North America, trauma causes about 25% of avalanche deaths. In 2009, Canadian mountain guide and emergency physician Jeff Boyd et al. found that trauma was a "significant contributing factor in a substantial proportion of asphyxia deaths." According to Dr. Boyd, major trauma was a contributor to one in three Canadian avalanche deaths, and in the deaths of one in two ice climbers. Because trauma is common in avalanche incidents, rescuers – whether companion or organized – should be ready to treat and care for injured victims.

Mechanisms of trauma include:
- a collision with trees, rocks, buildings and other objects
- a fall over cliffs or rough terrain
- being battered by a person's skis, snowboard, poles, snowshoes, etc.
- the compression of the snow

To treat trauma:
- conduct a thorough examination of the patient
- manage the airway and breathing
- control bleeding
- immobilize the spine, if indicated
- suspect head injuries
- splint fractures
- suspect internal injuries
- treat for shock
- monitor vital signs

Hypothermia

While hypothermia kills very few avalanche victims, hypothermia almost always affects those buried for any significant length of time. After a half hour, hypothermia should be considered almost certain, and for the survivor, treatment of hypothermia may become the most important medical action.

"Field rewarming" is a misnomer

because research has shown that adding heat is difficult; however, it is essential rescuers initiate immediate field rewarming to prevent additional cooling of the victim's core. Buried people can become significantly chilled after being uncovered and exposed to the elements. Rescuers should not completely uncover the victim until rescuers are able to protect their patient.

An exception is when the victim and rescuers must move away from a dangerous location. For example, a situation common in the rescue of ice climbers can occur when storm conditions or thaw conditions may cause reoccurring natural avalanches. Victims suspected of moderate to severe hypothermia must be handled gently to prevent initiating irregular heart rhythms.

In avalanche rescue, the old adage of "a hypothermic victim is not dead until they are warm and dead" requires modification to a more appropriate adage, "a hypothermic avalanche victim with an air pocket and an open airway is not dead until they are warm and dead."

Hypothermia may be characterized as:
- Mild
  - shivering
  - clumsiness, slow reactions, stumbling
  - mental confusion
  - difficulty speaking
  - "cold" to the touch
- Severe
  - cessation of shivering
  - unable to stand or walk
  - muscles become rigid
  - impaired responsiveness
  - dilated pupils
  - slow pulse and breathing
  - unresponsive and rigid

To treat hypothermia
- prevent further heat loss:
  - add insulation beneath and around the patient
  - shelter patient into a tent, shelter or wrap in a tarp
  - replace wet clothing with dry clothes (cover the head)
  - build a fire or start a stove.
- hydrate with warm, sweet liquids if patient is alert and able to swallow
- rewarm the patient as safely as possible (slow methods for severe hypothermia, fast and slow for mild hypothermia)
- try to reheat the core before the shell to prevent the return of "cold" blood to the core.

For mild hypothermia (core temperature above 90° F / 32.2° C, still shivering and mental status normal):
  - use warmed and humidified oxygen, if available
  - let patient shiver in a pre-warmed sleeping bag/blanket
  - place warmed water bottles or chemical heating pads on the neck, groin and sides of chest
  - use body-to-body warming in a pre-warmed sleeping bag
  - use warming devices such as a self-warming medical blanket, hydraulic sarong, electric blankets, charcoal heaters, etc.

For severe hypothermia (core temperature below 90° F / 32.2° C, not shivering, lowered mental status):
  - use warmed and humidified oxygen, if available
  - use extra caution and time – as long as two to three minutes – in assessing breathing and central pulse (carotid or femoral) before initiating cardio pulmonary resuscitation (CPR)
  - move *gently* during extrication and evacuations
  - prevent further cooling

- place warmed water bottles or chemical heating pads on the neck, groin and sides of chest
- use a pre-warmed sleeping bag or a self-warming medical blanket
- if CPR is initiated, continue CPR during transport if possible
- transport to advanced care as quickly as possible, preferably by helicopter

Extrication and packaging

When extricating a severely hypothermic patient, rescuers must use great care. All snow trapping the body must be removed so the patient can be removed as gently as possible. In addition to possible cardiac irritabilities, significant and rapid movements of a patient's limbs can cause an influx of cold blood from the periphery to flow into the core, which leads to additional cooling.

When repositioning a patient in severe hypothermia, his/her limbs should be moved slowly. When extricating the patient, be ready to immediately protect the patient from the environment. Snow is a great insulator, so be leery of causing more harm by unnecessarily exposing the person to cold and windy air. Consider initially exposing only the head and chest for the initial assessment, while others prepare some packaging materials.

When packaging, consider patient monitoring needs and wrap the patient in a warm, weatherproof manner that will keep out cold, wind, and snow or rain. Hard-working rescuers often do not realize how quickly their immobile patient gets cold. Also, dragging a rescue toboggan across snow tends to force snow into a patient's covers if not secured carefully.

Learning to transport a patient is best done on the hill where different techniques and equipment can be tried and tested. It is important to be experienced in the use of various toboggans, akjas, snowmobiles, etc. before using them in a rescue.

Multiple casualties

If several buried or injured victims must be cared for, the supportive care of the surviving victims takes priority over ones without vital signs. Careful consideration must be given when triaging and evacuating victims. Just because a rescue helicopter landed closer to one victim does not mean that this victim should be the first one evacuated. A victim with respiratory and airway problems should be transported first, before a victim in cardiac arrest. When resources are limited, the dictum, "save the savable" applies.

> **TIPS:**
> After extrication from the snow, rescuers must:
> • maintain an open airway
> • avoid rough handling or significant movements of the victim's body
> • avoid further heat loss

Cardiac problems

Cardiac problems can arise immediately from trauma to the heart or come later as a consequence of asphyxia or hypothermia.

Treatment of cardiac arrest includes CPR by trained personnel and quick transport of the victim to a hospital while continuing CPR. Don't stop resuscitation until directed by a physician or other legally-constituted authority (this can be done by a phone call or radio if needed).

Special techniques and equipment have been devised to allow CPR on rescue toboggans. The difficulty of performing CPR or other emergency care on a moving toboggan suggests another reason for getting a doctor or paramedic to the victim, and stabilizing the victim's condition before transporting. Performing CPR on a moving toboggan is especially difficult and takes planning, practice and sometimes special equipment.

Psychological emergency care

Avalanche incidents may result in serious injuries or even death, which create a strong emotional response resulting in psychological distress in victims, companions, and rescuers. When a person dies despite the hardworking efforts of rescuers, the stress can be significant. This immediate reaction should be seen as a normal response during the event and not a psychological problem.

However, without intervention, distress may develop into Acute Stress Disorder (ASD) and Post Traumatic Stress Disorder (PTSD). A small study in Europe showed that 28% of survivors suffered from acute PTSD and 18% developed chronic PTSD. Avalanche victims, companions and rescuers all may encounter changes in feelings, thoughts and behaviors.

In general, responding to an avalanche rescue or being involved in a serious incident is outside the norm of usual work or life experiences, so avalanche incidents may be called "critical incidents." Not all avalanche rescues will be critical incidents to every rescuer, but be aware that each rescuer will have a different reaction. Incidents that can result in stressful reactions to rescuers include significant trauma to the victim, incidents involving children, multiple victims, co-workers or friends, and incidents with a high degree of threat to rescuers. Two situations to address are the needs of rescuers and survivors during and after the operation.

During the operation

Mitigating psychological distress during the operation includes:

For the rescuer:
- accepting a rescuer's reaction; respecting and reassigning as needed
- checking in with fellow rescuers on an ongoing basis
- acknowledging one's own reactions.

For the survivor:
- sizing up the survivor's capabilities and putting the individual to work, if appropriate
- separating the individual from the group, if needed, and providing support
- informing survivors as to actions and future actions so they feel a part of the operation

A few survivors who are experiencing distress may act inappropriately, becoming irrational, loud, authoritative, or even belligerent with rescuers. They may show signs of exhaustion, they may minimize their own injuries, and they may experience faulty memories.

After the operation

To assist rescuers and others exposed to critical incidents, a systematic and comprehensive approach – Critical Incident Stress Management (CISM) – was developed in the late 1970s and early 1980s. CISM can be performed in a variety of methods; a common and simple approach is peer "defusing" when rescuers directly involved in the incident informally meet to discuss the event, address immediate needs, and offer a lifeline, typically a telephone number one can call to talk more. A defusing is done the day of the incident and may even be held at the Incident Site.

A few days later, usually within seventy-two hours, a formal debriefing called a Critical Incident Stress Debriefing (CISD) may be held. The debriefing is for those directly (on-site rescuers) and indirectly (operation leaders and support staff) involved to talk about the incident. The CISD often focuses on rescuers' feelings, coping methods, identifying those at risk, and informing rescuers of helpful resources within their community.

If unsure of available CISM resources, a call to local law enforcement will likely find trained leaders. Rescuers can also receive training or find trained leaders at the International Critical Stress Foundation, Inc. (icisf.org).

The efficacy of CISM and CISD is in dispute. After being used for decades, the empirical evidence of successful use of CISM and CISD for emergency responders seems strong. However, in recent years research done with victims shows CISM and CISD does not work and in some cases may even cause harm since it may resurrect past feelings.

Death

Some rescue responses may turn into a recovery effort and rescuers will deal with the recovery of a dead body. While only a physician or other legally-constituted authority can declare a victim dead, sometimes definitive or presumptive signs can help the rescuer know if death has occurred.

Presumptive signs may include a buried victim with no air pocket or an obstructed airway, or a rigid/frozen thorax. Be cautious about using burial time as a determinate, as buried avalanche victims have survived for more than twenty-four hours. When considering presumptive signs, usually some combination of signs is needed to pronounce death.

Definitive signs are obvious and include clear lethal injuries, dependent lividity, and a frozen body.

If death has occurred, the coroner or medical examiner must be notified. The body can only be moved at the direction of the coroner, or his or her legal delegate, such as a sheriff's officer. While awaiting instructions, it is important for rescuers to preserve the scene, and for rescuers to maintain their dignity and the dignity of the deceased, especially when family or friends have been participating in the search effort.

If the coroner is unable to travel to the avalanche Incident Site, rescuers should document the site, preferably with photographs. The body should be moved only after receiving authorization from the coroner.

• *Chapter Ten* •

Common Rescue Mistakes

Nearly half of all companion rescues are unsuccessful due to lack of adequate training, practice or equipment. Organized rescue efforts also exhibit mistakes that severely compromise the efficiency, if not the safety of the operation. No matter where, when, how or by whom the mistakes were made, they present vital lessons for all potential rescuers.

Mistakes made by rescuers can be grouped into five basic categories:
1) Poor organization
2) Mishandling the witness
3) Inadequate Immediate Search
4) Mismanaged search
5) Misconceptions

Poor organization

The five points below arise from a lack of organization and virtually guarantee chaos to some extent during the rescue.
- No plan or an unpracticed plan
- Leadership problems
- Communication problems
- Lack of proper equipment
- Failure to utilize available personnel

No plan or an unpracticed plan

Organizational problems generally arise from two sources: no plan or an unpracticed plan. In some cases, plans become out of date, so contact information for additional resources is incorrect resulting in needless delays. Both professional and

volunteer ski patrols and search and rescue groups need to have a written plan so that all members understand their potential role in any avalanche rescue. Controlling the chaos arising from rescues is one of the duties of the Incident Commander.

Leadership problems

Incident management problems arise quickly when leadership is weak, inexperienced or non-existent. Even experienced search and rescue managers have stumbled because they lacked experience with the nuances specific to avalanche rescue. Leadership problems typically result in unnecessary delays. While it is not known if any avalanche victim has died as a result of a poorly organized rescue operation, at least one rescuer has. In 1958, in Utah, a rescuer was buried and killed in a second avalanche after the rescue plan fell apart, and allowed responding teams to scatter on their way to the Incident Site. The same leadership mistakes continue to happen today but so far without these same tragic consequences.

Communication problems

Many of the mistakes described in this chapter can be traced to communication problems. Nothing can make a search and rescue operation completely fall apart faster than poor communication. Problems arise for technical and human reasons, and the likelihood of problems increases as the amount of preparation and practice decreases, or the number of organizations involved increases. Incompatible radio equipment has prevented many rescuers from hearing or reporting important information. Rugged terrain can easily prevent line-of-sight radio communications, so a radio relay may be needed. Prolonged cold, old batteries, and antenna problems have disabled many a radio and mobile phone. Practice and maintenance go a long way to ensure one's equipment is ready for all conditions.

Communication problems frequently occur for human reasons. Unclear and misunderstood messages have adversely affected many operations, and at times have put rescuers at risk. Messages that are not well thought out, clearly expressed or unconfirmed have caused confusion and delays. In addition, significant delays have occurred when information is not reported in a timely manner between the Incident Command and site operations. Leaders at the Command Post can only anticipate so much before they must rely on accurate information from the Incident Site. Likewise, leaders at the Incident Site need timely information about resources and support to keep the field operation running smoothly.

Miscommunications have occurred when specific-coded messages used by one organization were unknown or meant something completely different to another rescue team. For example, many rescue and law enforcement agencies use "Code 3" to indicate an emergency response; however, some organizations in emergency services use "Code 3" or "Priority 3" to indicate a non-emergency. Planning and executing any search and rescue operation requires excellent and timely communication between all parties involved. When unsure about the intent or meaning of a message, ask.

Lack of proper equipment

The lack of proper equipment or improperly used equipment, both rescue and personal, has slowed down many rescues or worse, has resulted in the death of rescuers. A rescue plan needs to specify where necessary rescue equipment is needed. That's why there is no substitute for an experienced, watchful eye making sure that individuals are properly equipped.

For rescues in or near developed areas, being well equipped is not nearly as critical as it is for rescuers going into the backcountry where forgotten or proper gear cannot be brought to them easily. For example, soft-soled boots such as snowmobile boots are perfect for probing but can be dangerous if climbing a steep, icy bed surface.

The lack of proper equipment certainly causes problems, but so too does the misuse of equipment. In recent years, several avalanche rescuers in Europe and Canada have unintentionally left their transceivers turned off or failed to turn their transceivers back on and were buried by a subsequent avalanche, either during the rescue effort or while returning to the Command Post.

Failure to utilize available personnel

Once again, a rescue plan helps in securing additional rescuers. The plan should list other available rescue groups, with at least two contact names and telephone numbers. Not long ago in Colorado during a backcountry avalanche search, one ski patrol failed to call in a second patrol, even though the first had only four members available and the second had twenty-eight members waiting less than twenty minutes away. It is far more prudent to request rescuers and then turn them back if needed, than to need them but not have called them. Incident Command must recognize the requirement for personnel early in the operation and the rescue plan needs to be up to date so additional rescuers can be contacted quickly.

Mishandling the witness

Typically, blame cannot be affixed to a witness but rather to the rescuers for how they interact, interview and interpret the words of the eyewitness.

In one extreme case, shortly after a large incident, a zealous sheriff told the press that the two eyewitnesses – who also triggered the slide that buried and killed four skiers – would be arrested and charged. Rumors hinted at felony manslaughter. Fearing the law, the two quickly went into hiding. It took more than a day to get the sheriff to back down from his threat, and to convince the witnesses to come forward and assist in the rescue. No charges were ever filed.

Common mistakes involving witnesses include the following:

- Failure to gather accurate information
- Failure to hold and question the witness
- Failure to return the witness to the original vantage point
- Failure to deal appropriately with an emotionally distraught witness
- Failure to keep track of the witness at the incident site

Inaccurate information

A rescuer might assume that a witness would never purposely give bad information, but experience and the record show it is not uncommon for witnesses to provide inaccurate information. Worse, in a very few number of incidents involving "closed" terrain at resorts, the reporting person has intentionally misreported the location, presumably to protect himself. The false information delayed rescue.

Poor interviewing skills on the part of the rescuer can be as much of a problem as an uncertain witness who did not carefully watch the incident. Rescuers asking close-ended questions – requiring yes or no answers – will get limited information.

Rescuers asking open-ended questions will get more information, often because the information will spur new questions.

As rescuers seek information it may be just as important for them to share information about how the rescue effort is progressing. When witnesses feel they are being helpful, whether by searching or providing information, they tend to become more personally involved and cooperative in the rescue.

The designation "last seen area" (LSA) is preferred over "last seen point" because of the potential for inaccurate information. Buried avalanche victims have been found above or well to the side of what was formerly called the last seen point, out of the anticipated flow line. The LSA is a good place to begin to look for other clues that might support the witness's story, but rescuers should be alert to clues that indicate inaccuracies in the witness's observations.

One of the first questions asked by a rescuer is, "How many people are buried?" What seems like a simple question, requiring one simple answer, is not always so easy. Inaccurate counts often arise when a witness does not personally know the victims or did not witness the entire slide. This typically occurs when a person witnesses an incident from a distance, one that occurs to another group or the reporting person does not know his/her companions well, as might be the case on a mountain-club tour. The point is that when the witness knows his/her companions, the witness pays closer attention to where they are on the slope, knows how many there are, and knows who is accounted for and who is not.

Obviously, the witness(es) should be questioned about their relationship with the possible victims. Rescues have ended prematurely, only to have the rescuers called back hours later to search for and then find someone who was reported missing later in the day. If there is any question as to the number of victims, search the entire debris area.

Failure to hold and question the witness

Today, most reports of avalanche incidents are made from mobile phones to 911 call centers rather than a face-to-face meeting with a ski patroller or rescuer. Both methods still produce problems. For 911 call takers, the rescue response can be initiated more effectively when the call taker has an avalanche-specific incident form from which to ask relevant questions. Since avalanche incidents are infrequent, it is helpful for rescue agencies to work with their local call center to prepare a list of need-to-know questions. Most call centers can now transfer the call directly to the local ski patrol or other rescue team, which can reduce mistakes caused by relaying messages. If not, rescue teams should be sure to get a callback number for the reporting person and should contact this person immediately.

The rescue response can be helped significantly if the 911 call taker asks the reporting person not to move from their position until they speak with a rescuer. Too often, cell phone connections are lost when someone descends below a ridge-line. A reporting party can be asked for GPS coordinates. When feasible, assign someone to meet with and keep track of the witness(es). Witnesses provide the best source of information and it is important to keep them available. Always try to obtain and write down names, addresses, and telephone numbers of all witnesses.

A new wrinkle in the alerting process is the use of automated distress signals from personal locator beacons (PLBs) and satellite locators (SPOT). The push of a button on these small devices sends an automated signal, including GPS location, to a satellite, which is then picked up by a monitor-ing service that relays the distress call to an emergency service center closest to the location of the device. It provides quick notification of an emergency, but not necessarily the nature of the emergency. If a signal is reported and the location indicated is in avalanche terrain with significant hazard, an avalanche incident should be presumed unless or until it is ruled out by other information.

Failure to return the witness to the original vantage point

Getting the witness back to the same vantage point is critical for getting accurate information. A witness trying to identify tracks or locate the LSA from somewhere other than the spot he/she saw the incident will be much more prone to make mistakes. It will require extra effort, but rescuers must get the witness back to the original viewpoint as soon as possible.

Failure to deal appropriately with an emotionally distraught witness

Generally, companions or witnesses give good information and are very willing and able to assist in the rescue effort. Rarely have witness(es) been too emotionally distraught to provide good information or assistance to rescuers. However, rescuers should anticipate the companion's emotional change once the victim has been found and the outcome does not look favorable. Rescuers should be ready to support and comfort the companion(s). A grieving or upset person requires a great deal of comfort and support. Today, many law enforcement agencies can provide a victim's advocate who can help companions and the victim's family.

Failure to keep track of the witness

When a witness disappears, so too does potentially critical information. For instance, identifying ownership of clues can lead to the realization that there are more victims buried than previously thought.

A witness at a ski resort slipped away for more skiing. In this case, the missing witness caused only a minor inconvenience to the search operation because the search area was very small.

In other instances, the consequences caused delays in the search effort. On at least one occasion, the consequences turned deadly. During a rescue many years ago, an eyewitness wandered away from rescuers at the Incident Site. Hours later, the witness, a boy, was found dead from hypothermia less than a mile away.

Inadequate Immediate Search

Immediate Search actions are those performed by the first rescuers who reach the victim's companions and/or witnesses to the avalanche. The clock is ticking on buried victims, and mistakes truly may have deadly consequences.

Here are five types of Immediate Search mistakes:
- No Immediate Search
- Inadequate searching – missing visual clues
- Lack of proficiency with avalanche rescue beacons
- Not listening for the victim's voice
- Not finding the Incident Site

No Immediate Search

An Immediate Search is absolutely necessary and is the most likely means of achieving a live rescue. If no immediate search is made, there is no chance of finding and helping a victim. Companions need to search before going for help. A 911 call, radio call or activation of a satellite distress beacon should be attempted right away. Organized rescue teams should also conduct an Immediate Search before starting probe lines.

Inadequate search

In numerous incidents, members of the party left the avalanche without doing a thorough Immediate Search, missing visual clues that might otherwise help save a life. In December 1984, two backcountry skiers were caught in a slide near Aspen, Colorado. The survivor dug herself out, made a hasty check of the debris, and left the site to notify rescuers. Hours later, an Immediate Search by a small team of rescuers revealed a ski tip sticking from the snow. The victim, shallowly buried, had died. Almost every year this same sort of scenario occurs.

Organized rescue teams also have done inadequate Immediate Searches by not searching the entire area before starting probe lines. Only later, as the probe lines moved up the debris, did rescuers spot an obvious ski or ski pole sticking out of the snow.

A few years ago a skier-triggered avalanche dumped snow onto a Colorado highway. The Immediate Search consisted only of a beacon search. With easy access, numerous rescuers arrived quickly and probe lines were begun immediately on the roadway so the highway could be opened as quickly as possible. Only later were the likely burial areas, about two dozen different trees, searched. Somehow, the search priorities were rearranged from looking for a person to opening the road. Fortunately, no one was found in the slide.

If the Immediate Search fails to turn up enough clues to establish the likely burial areas, rescuers should consider redoing the Immediate Search. The better the clues, the smaller the area rescuers must probe. Once probe lines begin, the speed of any search slows dramatically.

Lack of proficiency with avalanche transceivers

Avalanche transceivers are lifesavers but even the newest technology requires practice, practice, and more practice. On New Year's Day 2000, two backcountry skiers were caught; one was able to dig himself out and began a transceiver search. No signal was detected. A severe storm forced the survivor to retreat to a mountain hut for two days before going for help. It turned out that the survivor was using a borrowed, unfamiliar transceiver and unknowingly switched it from "send" to "off" instead of to "receive."

In February 2005, an avalanche buried a backcountry skier. Several companions attempted a transceiver search, but got hopelessly confused. After nearly a half hour of fruitless searching, one of the group placed a 911 call and was immediately patched in to a local ski patrol. (The Incident Site was visible from a lift terminal.) Based on questions asked and answers given, the patroller taking the call was able to determine that more than one transceiver was still transmitting and the rescuers were unknowingly tracking each other. After getting that situation under control, companions were still not able to conduct an effective search. Ultimately, the patroller had the calling party hold his transceiver close to the cell phone. The patroller then directed the transceiver search remotely, using the audible tones. Unfortunately, the victim did not survive.

Some newer transceivers automatically turn back to transmit after a set period of time. This auto-revert function, intended as a safety feature, can cause confusion when not recognized.

Luck was with a group of four backcountry skiers in Colorado in 1988 when a small slide completely buried three. The group was well equipped – all had transceivers and shovels – but only one of the members was trained and practiced in transceiver use. Two others in the group had very limited training while the fourth had no training whatsoever. It was this fourth member who

was not caught in the slide. Relying on instincts rather than the transceiver, he quickly spotted a hand protruding from the snow and dug out the most experienced member, who then used his transceiver to find the other two buried skiers. They survived, and today all four are very proficient with avalanche rescue transceivers.

Not listening for the victim

Remember to listen while searching. Dozens of shallowly-buried avalanche victims have been recovered when rescuers heard yells coming from the snow. In one case in Utah, a tired shoveler moved away from the search area to rest. The buried victim, still conscious, heard the man and yelled. The startled rescuer alerted the others. The victim was soon freed after a four-hour burial.

Inadequate information about the location of the Incident Site

Incomplete questioning has misled a number of rescuers. Some Immediate Search Teams have wasted considerable amounts of time trying to get to an Incident Site because of vague or poor directions.

Careful questioning and witness management might reveal the easiest and safest access for the Immediate Search Team to reach the Incident Site. Even with a coherent witness, locating an Incident Site in stormy weather can be difficult; nightfall might make it impossible.

Mismanaged search

Serious mistakes have resulted in prolonged operations:
- Not searching the entire debris
- Not searching the toe
- Not digging where dogs alert
- Contaminating the avalanche debris
- Staging on the avalanche

Not searching the entire debris

Unintentionally missing or deliberately skipping parts of an avalanche have caused more than a few rescue efforts to go on much longer than needed. Imagine the surprise of one highway department heavy-equipment operator who was clearing a road and unexpectedly found a buried station wagon. The driver of the car was lucky, having been buried eight hours and now saved more by providence than by plan. Rescuers, hours earlier, had probed part of the debris and stopped after prematurely deciding that no vehicles were buried.

Not searching the toe

Numerous rescue efforts have been stymied because the toe (or end) of the avalanche was ignored. Victims or clues, like backpacks, ski poles, and other gear, often end up near or at the end of the debris, especially when the victim was caught or struck low on the slope. These clues were missed for hours and in some cases days, which only delayed the search effort. In other cases, probe lines were not started at the toe of the debris. Perhaps there was some clue that warranted searching higher up, but in several cases, the victims were later found in the toe of the debris. In a few unusual cases, avalanche victims were driven under the undisturbed snow a few meters beyond the obvious end of the debris.

Not digging where dogs alert

The nose of a trained avalanche dog is one of the more efficient search tools. On several occasions, dogs alerted only to be pulled away because the spot was not where the human rescuers expected to find a buried victim. Also, rescuers must remember a rescue dog finds scent, and that scent may or may not be directly above the buried victim. The scent seeks the path of least resistance as it rises to the surface.

Avalanche debris that covers brush, trees, an open creek or lake, the wreckage of a building, or even blocks of a hard slab may cause the victim's scent to percolate upwards some distance away from the actual position. Though the dog alerts at a single point on the surface, rescuers should probe the surrounding area.

Contamination of the avalanche debris

Contamination problems arise from the actions of sloppy rescuers at the site of an avalanche, resulting in the misidentification of clues. If it is not possible to get a rescue dog to the Incident Site with the first wave of rescuers, it is important to keep the debris area clean. Do not allow rescuers to throw food scraps, spit tobacco, relieve themselves, or sit on the debris. The added scents make the dog's job very difficult. Even when rescuers are clean, a dropped hat or a set-aside jacket may cause confusion for other rescuers who may mistake the mislaid gear for a clue.

Staging on the avalanche debris

In a number of searches, the Staging Area was placed on the debris, or with time, the area gradually crept up onto the debris. Sadly, in a few cases, victims ended up being beneath unknowing rescuers.

Misconceptions

Many circumstances can conspire against avalanche victims to keep organized rescuers away. High avalanche hazard, vicious weather, and precarious terrain are beyond the control of rescuers and can doom a victim, but rescuers can control their attitudes upon which they make decisions. Misconceptions by rescuers about survival and search technologies do no favors for victims and rescuers alike, and in a few cases have likely worsened the fate of the buried victim.

To avoid:
- Hasty generalization that rescue teams find only dead bodies
- Reluctance to adopt new technologies

Hasty generalization that rescue teams find only dead bodies

An often-heard statement from avalanche educators is, "Organized rescue only finds dead bodies." This presumption reduces the chances of the buried victim who might be the lucky one to survive a long burial. This statement tragically becomes self-fulfilling when believed by rescuers. Of course, all rescuers must follow the golden rule of rescue – do not make the incident worse – and must carefully assess and manage risks. Several search efforts have been ended as night fell for the convenience of rescuers. Instead, rescuers are reminded that because some buried victims do survive for many hours, no avalanche victim should ever be denied this small chance at life. Another way to look at the situation is to consider what a victim would want rescuers to do.

Reluctance to adopt new technologies

In the 1960s and early 1970s, trained avalanche rescue dogs were seen as a novelty or even as superfluous by some. When it was demonstrated that one rescue dog could do the job of 100 probers, some rescue leaders were still slow to use dogs or even support the training of more dogs. Today training and deployment of rescue dogs is strongly encouraged and numbers are growing.

Until the early 1980s, avalanche rescue transceivers were thought of as a tool only for avalanche professionals and not for recreationists. Today transceivers are de rigueur for everyone traveling in avalanche terrain.

In the 1990s, many rescuers (and casual recreationists) scoffed at mobile telephone use in the backcountry. Now emergency service programs around the world praise the value of mobile phones in saving lives.

Even today, many rescuers are slow to adopt proven technologies, such as hand-held radar systems, where one unit can do the work of hundreds of rescuers.

Rescuers should realize that no one technology is better than another, because the circumstances of avalanche incidents always differ. Each technology should be thought of as another tool in the rescuer's toolbox, and just like a carpenter, the more tools available, the easier and faster the job. Rescuers are reminded not to focus only on how people have been found in the past, but to think of how technology might help find someone tomorrow.

Appendices

APPENDIX A

SAMPLE EQUIPMENT LIST

Immediate Search Team
Personal Equipment
- Transceiver
- Probe
- Shovel
- Radio
- Personal gear appropriate for conditions (see personal gear for off-area rescue below)

Rescue Equipment:
- Rescue dog, if available
- RECCO detector, if available
- Cell phone
- Small medical kit
- Flagging/wands (red, blue and yellow)
- Flagging/surveyor's tape, different colors
- GPS, map and compass
- Small pruning saw
- Digital camera
- Spare clothing for victim(s)

Additional Teams
- Personal equipment listed above
- Fixed-length probes
- Guide cords
- Sturdy shovels

Medical Team
- Airway kit
- Oxygen
- Suction
- Automated External Defibrillator (AED)
- Backboard/Vacuum-splint mattress
- Blankets/Sleeping bag
- Chemical hot packs
- Splints
- Trauma kit
- Thermometer (hypothermia)
- Tarp or other shelter
- Advanced Life Support kit/Physician kit (see NSP *Outdoor Emergency Care* (OEC) manual)
- Pulse-oximeter
- IVs

Transport/Evacuation Team
- Toboggan, sled or litter
- Snowmobile hitch for toboggan/sled
- Rescue rope(s) for lowering or hauling
- Basic lowering and hauling hardware

Site Gear/Support Gear
- Large tent
- Stove/cook kit
- Message pads and pencils
- Communications board, pin-up notice pads
- Megaphone
- Extra probes
- Extra shovels
- Extra wands/flagging
- Colored cord
- Generator and fuel
- Lights
- Flares
- Portable heaters
- Folding table(s)
- Folding chairs
- Chainsaw(s)
- Porta-potty or privacy screening material for latrine
- Toilet paper/hand cleaner

Personal Gear: Off-Area
- AT/Telemark skis and skins, or snowshoes
- Spare clothing
- Spare gloves/mittens
- Chemical hot packs
- Food and water, Thermos
- Lighter and fire starter
- Whistle
- Headlamp
- Bivouac shelter

APPENDIX B

SAMPLE PERSONNEL CONTACT SHEET

Designation	Name	Telephone
Area Personnel		
Incident Commander		
Site Leader		
Area Manager		
Mountain Operations		
Incident Dispatcher		
Lift Operations		
Ski School		
Resort Food Services		
Public Affairs		
First Aid Room/Clinic		
Off-Area Contacts		
Sheriff		
Other Law Enforcement		
Park Service (in Nat. Park)		
Forest Service		
Fire Department		
Ambulance		
Hospital		
Helicopter		
Dog/Handler		
RECCO Detector (if not on site)		
Other Ski Patrol		
Other Ski Patrol		
Search & Rescue Group		
Search & Rescue Group		
Mobile Canteen		
Local Avalanche Center		

APPENDIX C

SAMPLE WITNESS INTERVIEW SHEET

(Prepare a separate report for each witness)

Interviewer Name _____

Date _____   Time of Report _____

Witness:

Name _____ Age _____

Address _____

Telephone: Primary (   ) _____   Secondary (   ) _____

Description of incident:

Time _____ Location _____

_____

_____

_____

_____

_____

_____

_____

_____

_____

_____

_____

Number of Persons: Caught _____ Injured _____ Buried _____

APPENDIX C, CONTINUED

Description of Buried/Missing Persons		
Name/ Gender/Age	Description (clothing / pack color, transceiver, travel gear, etc.)	Known to Witness (Y/N)

APPENDIX C, CONTINUED

Group's route to incident site

Relative positions of subjects when caught (if possible, sketch the incident site)

Actions taken by companions

Witness's route out of site/condition of route

Witness's ability to return to site

Disposition of Witness

___ Witness escorted to site: Time _____ Escort _____

___ Witness escorted to base for further information/care/release: Time _____

Escort _____

APPENDIX D
SAMPLE CHECKLIST/DATA FORM

The person to first receive a report of an avalanche incident assumes the Incident Commander (IC) role, but the position usually transfers quickly to a pre-designated leader. During prolonged rescue operations, this position may shift between two or more people without compromising operational continuity. This checklist/form helps to provide a digest of data gathered and actions taken to support that continuity.

IC Identification
Name _____

Assumed Command: Date _____ Time _____

Relieved by: Name _____ Date _____ Time _____

Relieved by: Name _____ Date _____ Time _____

Relieved by: Name _____ Date _____ Time _____

Initial Information
Incident reported: Date_____ Time_____ By whom _____

Incident Data: Number of persons caught _____ Time _____

Location _____

_____

Time personnel alerted: _____

Witness interviewer/escort _____(see Witness Interview Sheet)

Initial Leadership/Staff Assignments (leave blank until assigned)
Operations Chief
Name _____ Time _____

Immediate Search Team Leader _____

Team name/number_____ Roster given to _____

RECCO_____ Dog team handler _____

Site Leader_____ Time _____

Dispatcher _____ Time _____

Scribe _____ Time _____

Medical Team Leader _____ Time _____

Team name/number _____ Roster given to_____

Evacuation Team Leader _____ Time _____

Team name/number _____ Roster given to_____

APPENDIX D, CONTINUED

Notifications

Area Management _____ Time _____

Authorities (varies by area)_____ Time _____

Closures/Guides

Lifts closed _____

_____

Areas (runs) closed _____

Guards to restrict access to authorized personnel only

Name_____ Location _____

Name_____ Location _____

Guides to escort authorized personnel

Name_____ Location _____

Name_____ Location _____

Hazard mitigation

Leader name_____ Team name/number _____

Roster given to _____

Communications network

Radio frequencies/channels _____

_____

Emergency Medical Agencies on standby

Ambulance _____ Helicopter_____

Hospital_____

Staging and check-in for arriving rescue teams and volunteers

_____

Other Command and General Staff positions as needed per ICS

Safety Officer _____ Time _____

Public Information Officer _____ Time _____

Liaison Officer _____ Time _____

Logistics Chief _____ Time _____

Planning Chief _____ Time _____

Wrap up of operations (may be done by Planning Chief)

• Check-in personnel and equipment_____

• Put equipment back in service _____

• Gather paperwork _____

• Debrief _____

APPENDIX E

SAMPLE IC SCRIBE NOTES

This is a page that can be used for keeping track of immediate events and actions until the Scribe has access to record-keeping forms specified in the rescue plan.

Incident Data

Notification date & time _____

Approximate incident date & time _____

Incident location _____

_____

Total number of people involved _____ Number buried _____

Witness(es)

Name(s) _____

    address_____ phone _____

Name(s) _____

    address_____ phone _____

Name(s) _____

    address_____ phone _____

Notifications:

Entity _____Person _____Time _____

Entity _____Person _____Time _____

Entity _____Person _____Time _____

Initial Leadership (designated person & time):

Incident Commander _____Time _____

Operations Chief _____Time _____

APPENDIX E, CONTINUED

Logistics Chief _____Time _____

Dispatcher _____Time _____

Immediate Search team leader _____Time _____

Site leader _____Time _____

Medical team leader _____Time _____

Others:

_____Time _____

_____Time _____

_____Time _____

_____Time _____

Operational Status

Immediate search team departure time _____ Arrival time _____

Initial Status of Incident Site _____

_____

_____

_____

_____

_____

_____

Persons Found

Name_____ Time _____Condition _____

Name_____ Time _____Condition _____

Name_____ Time _____Condition _____

APPENDIX F

SAMPLE DISPATCH LOG

Team Designation	Leader	Destination	Number of Personnel	Time of Departure	Time of Arrival	Time of Return

APPENDIX G

SAMPLE TEAM ROSTER

(To be left behind with staging area leader upon dispatch)

Team designation _____

Leader _____Radio #_____Channel/frequency _____
Cell phone number_____

Members/Specialty (M.D., evacuation., etc.)

_____

_____

_____

_____

_____

_____

_____

Team Equipment _____

_____

_____

_____

_____

_____

Time Dispatched _____ Destination _____

_____

Time of Departure _____ Time returned to base _____

SELECTED REFERENCES

American Psychiatric Association. "First aid for psychological reactions in disasters." Washington, DC. 1964.

Armstrong, Betsy R. and Knox T. Williams. *The Avalanche Book,* second edition. Golden, Colo.: Fulcrum Publishing, 1992.

Atkins, Dale. "The probe efficiency index and better ways to do the coarse probe." *The Avalanche Review.* 18(3): 10–12, 2000.

Ballard, Henry, Lin Ballard and Dale Atkins. "Probing for avalanche victims." Proceedings of the International Snow Science Workshop: 343–348. Jackson, Wyo. Sept. 19–24, 2004.

Ballard, Henry, Lin Ballard and Dale Atkins. "Probing for avalanche victims revisited." Proceedings of the International Snow Science Workshop: 579-583. avalanche.org/~issw. /issw_previous/2006/proceedings/data/papers/091.pdf.Telluride, Colo. Oct. 1-6, 2006.

Bowman, Warren D., MD. and David H. Johe, MD. *Outdoor Emergency Care,* fourth edition. Sudbury, Mass: Jones and Bartlett Publishers, 2003.

Boyd, Jeff, Pascal Haegeli, Riyad Abu-Laban, Michael Shuster, John C. Butt. "Patterns of death among avalanche fatalities: a 21-year review." *Canadian Medical Association Journal,* 180 (5).; doi:10.1503/cmaj.081327. March 3, 2009, first published February 12, 2009.

Brugger, Hermann. "Should strategies for care of avalanche victims change?" *Canadian Medical Association Journal,* commentary, doi:10.1503/cmaj.090085. March 2009.

Brugger Hermann, Guenther Sumann and Roland Meister et al. "Hypoxia and hypercapnia during respiration into an artificial air pocket in snow: Implications for avalanche survival." *Resuscitation.* 58:81–88. July 2003.

Bryson, Sandy. *Search and Rescue Dog Training,* Pacific Grove, Calif.: The Boxwood Press, 1976.

Burnett, Patti. *Avalanche Hasty Search: The Care and Training of Avalanche Search and Rescue Dogs,* Phoenix, Ariz.: Doral Publishing, 2003.

Daffern, Tony. *Avalanche Safety for Skiers, Climbers, and Snowboarders,* second revised edition. Calgary, Alberta: Rocky Mountain Books, 1999.

Edgerly, Bruce and Dale Atkins. "Strategic shoveling: The next frontier in companion rescue." Proceedings of the International Snow Science Workshop: 579-583. Telluride, Colo. October 1-6, 2006.

Elsensohn, Fidel, ed. "Consensus guidelines on mountain emergency medicine and risk reduction," International Commission for Alpine Rescue – Medcom. Casa Editrice Stefanoni – Lecco. 2001.

Falk, Markus, Hermann Brugger, H.; Lisolette Adler-Kastner. "Avalanche survival chances," *Nature.* 368 (6466): 21. 1994.

Forgey, William, ed. *Wilderness Medical Society: Practice Guidelines for Wilderness Emergency Care,* fifth edition. Guilford, Conn.: Falcon Guides, The Globe Pequot Press. 2006.

Fraser, Colin. *The Avalanche Enigma,* New York, N.Y. Rand McNally & Company. 1966.

Fredston, Jill and Doug Fesler. *Snow Sense: A Guide to Evaluating Snow Avalanche Hazard,* fifth edition. Anchorage, Alaska: Alaska Mountain Safety Center, Inc., 1999.

Fredston, Jill. *Snowstruck: In the Grip of Avalanches,* Orlando, Fla.: Harcourt Inc. 2005.

Genswein, Manuel and Ragnhild Eide. "V-shaped conveyor-belt approach to snow transport," *The Avalanche Review.* February 2008.

Hohlrieder, Matthias et al. "Rescue missions for totally buried avalanche victims: Conclusions from 12 years of experience," *High Altitude Medicine & Biology,* volume 9, number 3. Mary Ann Liebert, Inc. 2008.

Hohlrieder Matthias; Stephanie Thaler; Walter Wuertl, Wolfgang Voelckel; Hanno Ulmer; Hermann Brugger; and Peter Mair. "Rescue missions for totally buried avalanche victims: Conclusions from 12 years of experience," *High Altitude Medicine & Biology.* 9 (3). 2008.

Johe, David, MD. "Time is of the essence: OEC for avalanche victims," *Ski Patrol Magazine,* 19(2): 68-69. 2003.

Johnson, Sidney Morris, MD; Adam Clark Johnson; and Richard Barton, MD. "Avalanche trauma and closed head injury: Adding insult to injury," *Wilderness Environmental Medicine,* 12(4): 244-247. 2001.

LaChapelle, Edward. *The ABC of Avalanche Safety,"* third edition. Seattle, Wash.: The Mountaineers. 2003.

Laney, Mike. *Avalanche Rescue Quick Guide,* 2009 edition, Lakewood, Colo.: National Ski Patrol System, Inc. 2009.

Logan, Nick and Dale Atkins. *The Snowy Torrents: Avalanche Accidents in the United States 1980-1986,* Denver, Colo.: Colorado Geological Survey, Department of Natural Resources. 1996.

McCammon, Ian; Michael Ditolla and Scott McIntosh, MD. "Terrain and traumatic injury in U.S. avalanche accidents," Proceedings of the International Snow Science Workshop. Whistler, B.C. Sept. 21-27: 238-243, issw2008.com/papers/P8120.pdf. 2008.

McClung, David and Peter Schaerer. *The Avalanche Handbook,* third edition. Seattle, Wash.: The Mountaineers. 2006.

Oberhammer, Rosmarie; Werner Beikircher; Christoph Hörmann; Ingo Lorenz; Roger Pycha; Liselotte Adler-Kastner and Hermann Brugger. "Full recovery of an avalanche victim with profound hypothermia and prolonged cardiac arrest treated by extracorporeal re-warming." *Resuscitation* 76(3): 474-480. 2008.

Perla, Ronald and Martinelli, M., Jr. *Avalanche Handbook.* U.S. Department of Agriculture, Forest Service, Agriculture Handbook 489. 1976.

Snow, Weather, and Avalanches: Observational Guidelines for Avalanche programs in the United States. Pagosa Springs, Colo.: The American Avalanche Association. 2009.

Stopper, Dieter; Franz Hohensinn and Bruce Edgerly. "Searching in parallel: Harnessing manpower in transceiver rescues." Proceedings of the International Snow Science Workshop, Davos, Switzerland. Sept. 27 to Oct. 2: 671–674. 2009.

Tremper, Bruce. *Staying Alive in Avalanche Terrain,* second edition. Seattle, Wash.: The Mountaineers. 2008.

Wechsberg, Joseph. *Avalanche.* Alfred A. Knopf, Inc. New York, N.Y. 1958.

Williams, Knox and Betsy Armstrong. *The Snowy Torrents: Avalanche Accidents in the United States 1972-1979.* Jackson, Wyo.: Teton Bookshop Publishing. 1984.

About the Authors

Dale Atkins is a long-time mountain rescuer. He has worked as a professional ski patroller and avalanche forecaster/researcher and has participated in over three dozen avalanche rescues. Dale instructs avalanche rescue around the world, and he represents United States as the co-chairman of the International Commission for Alpine Rescue (ICAR) Avalanche Rescue Commission. He also chairs the Search and Rescue Committee of the American Avalanche Association.

Lin Ballard served as the NSP National Avalanche Program Supervisor for five years during which she wrote the first NSP *Avalanche Instructor Manual*. She is the recipient of the Monty M. Atwater Award for Avalanche Education and was recognized at the 2008 International Snow Science Workshop for work in the avalanche field by the Avalanche Divas. She is currently an avalanche instructor trainer for the NSP's Rocky Mountain Division.

Lin and Dale have collaborated on several projects including rescue research papers, magazine articles, and educational rescue videos.